In Sickness As In Health

*Helping Couples Cope
with the Complexities of Illness*

Barbara Kivowitz and Roanne Weisman

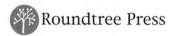Roundtree Press

www.insicknessasinhealth.com

About the Authors:

Roanne Weisman is an award-winning medical/science author of seven trade health books published by McGraw-Hill and Harvard Medical School, as well as Health Communications, Inc. Her co-authors include faculty of Harvard Medical School and leading academic medical centers. Her feature stories have appeared in magazines including *Prevention, Country Living, Alternative Medicine,* and *Body and Soul,* as well as magazines of Massachusetts General Hospital and Beth Israel Deaconess Medical Center, both teaching institutions of Harvard Medical School. She also writes regularly for online health education sites. She is the principal of Words That Work, which provides communications consulting and editorial services to large organizations.

Barbara Kivowitz, MSW, is a psychotherapist and consultant. She worked as a therapist in a community mental health center and as an advisor to a hospice program and has had experience helping couples facing illness. In addition, she has authored several articles on couples and illness and on living with pain, one of which was published in *Women's Day* and another in the journal of the American Pain Foundation. She is the co-author of *The Manager's Pocket Guide to Knowledge Management*, published by HRD Press. Since 2007 she has blogged about couples and illness at www. InSicknessInHealth.blogspot.com. Her blog has been nominated for best literary blog and best patient blog. She is on the board of trustees of Harvard Vanguard Medical Associates. She has a graduate degree from Harvard University in Romance Languages and Literatures.

We want to thank the experts who shared their knowledge and time with us and those whose works we consulted:

The Reverend Canon Nancy Adams, B.A., M.Div., *Anglican priest*

Julietta Appleton, MPA, CLC, CHT, *certified life coach and hypnotherapist, expert in human sexuality*

Helen Battler, M.Div., *spiritual care specialist*

David Bohm, Ph.D., *quantum physicist and philosopher*

Reverend Gwen Langdoc Buehrens, *priest in the Episcopal Church, grief counselor, and hospice worker*

Reverend John Buehrens, *former president of the Unitarian Universalist Association and currently a Unitarian Universalist church minister*

Abby Caplin, M.D., M.A., *physician, specialist in mind-body medicine and counseling*

Pierre Faubert, *Jungian psychologist*

Rabbi Gedaliah Fleer, *expert in the ancient traditions of Judaism and Jewish mysticism*

Ruth Lipman, Ph.D., *research associate with the Foundation for Informed Medical Decision Making*

H. Eugene Lindsey, Jr., M.D., *cardiologist, and president and CEO of Atrius Health, Inc., and of Harvard Vanguard Medical Associates*

Salvatore Maddi, Ph.D., *psychologist, professor, and founder of the Hardiness Institute*

Suzanne McCarthy, Psy.D., *psychologist and researcher*

Xiao Ming Cheng, L. Ac., *scholar and practitioner of traditional Chinese medicine*

Kathy Platoni, Psy.D., *clinical psychologist, colonel U.S. Army Reserve, Army Reserve Psychology Consultant to the Chief, Medical Service Corp*

Ester Shapiro, Ph.D., *psychologist, researcher, professor, and author*

Tulku Thondup Rinpoche, *visiting scholar at Harvard University and expert in Tibetan Buddhism*

Carol Wogrin, Psy.D., R.N., *director of the National Center for Death Education*

Byron Woodman, Jr., J.D. L.L.M., *estate planning lawyer*

Janna Zwerner, M.R.C., L.R.C., C.R.C. *chief of staff of the Massachusetts Rehabilitation Commission*

In Sickness As In Health:
Helping Couples Cope with the Complexities of Illness

Copyright © 2013 Barbara Kivowitz and Roanne Weisman

Jacket design by Iain R. Morris

ISBN: 978-1-93735-913-3

Printed in the United States of America
10 9 8 7 6 5 4 3 2 1

Roundtree Press
6 Petaluma Blvd. North, Suite B-6
Petaluma, CA 94952

www.roundtreepress.com

*I thank my life partner, my husband Richard, whose unwavering love,
selflessness, and commitment to me and my capacity for healing
still astound me. (BK)*

*To my children, Benjamin and Elizabeth, and my daughter-in-love, Lindsey,
for the depth of love and profound healing that we continue to share.
The joy that you have brought into my life makes
everything worthwhile. (RW)*

Acknowledgments

It would not be an exaggeration to say that writing this book was a healing experience for us. We are both writers. Roanne's focus is science, biomedicine, and health; Barbara was a clinical psychotherapist for many years and is now a business consultant. We have each had our own journeys from illness to health within our relationships. By listening to couples, surviving partners, and experts tell their stories, we expanded our sense of what is possible when self-awareness, intelligence, and compassion (toward others and toward oneself) are brought to bear on the experience of illness or disability. When a couple talked about their joys and struggles, or an expert described ways of transcending illness, we learned how to expand our awareness, not only beyond the constraints of our own experiences with illness, but into a fuller life after illness.

We have many people to thank for this. With great appreciation and humility, we thank all the couples and surviving partners who told us their stories with courage and authenticity. We also gratefully thank the experts from so many different disciplines who shared their wisdom with such candor and clarity.

This book would not have been possible without the heartfelt commitment and substantial efforts of our wonderful literary agent, Rebecca Gradinger, our powerful marketing team, Bridget Kinsella, Pat Walsh, Rochelle Lefkowitz, and our publisher, Cameron + Company.

- Barbara Kivowitz and Roanne Weisman

Table of Contents

Introduction

When you fell in love, what were you thinking? Perhaps you weren't thinking very much at all, because you were engulfed by feelings and dreams: by the soaring passions of romance and chemistry, by palpitating hearts and eager hands, by the promise of a joyful future with your loved one by your side. You and your partner may have pledged privately, or in front of witnesses, to love and honor each other "for better or for worse, in sickness and in health." In all likelihood, however, neither of you gave much thought to the "for worse" or "in sickness" parts of that loving contract.

And who could blame you? It is our very disregard for what might go wrong that permits us to carry on normally in a world filled with hazards. Were we to acknowledge the frailty of life at every moment, we would either be enlightened or immobilized by fear. For most of us, it is our assumption of relative predictability, safety, and longevity that permits us to take pleasure in our daily lives. We move from day to day believing that the ground we tread on will not give way; that we will have two legs on which to continue walking; a sound mind to direct us; and enough breath to cover the distance.

"No One Gets Through this Life Alive"

However, things do not always go as we plan. A feisty grandmother we know once said, "No one gets through this life alive." One day, amid the comforting chaos of careers, children, finances, groceries, extended family, new shoes, dental cleanings, and laundry, something might happen—or perhaps something has already happened—in your relationship. One of you may become sick, or receive a frightening diagnosis, or be injured. For some couples, catastrophic trauma arrives without warning. For others, what began as a headache, tiredness, difficulty breathing, a skin rash, confusion, or an unfamiliar lump can be the starting point for the furtive creep of chronic illness or pain.

For couples, illness is never a solo flight. When one partner is sick, both lives are dislocated. Whether the illness enters insidiously or announces itself with the sudden blast of a catastrophe, it fractures all of the couple's familiar patterns and forces them to drill down to the bedrock of their relationship and decide where they stand. Some couples break apart; others stay together but assume profoundly different roles. Some despair; others find renewed commitment and meaning.

The ill person may suddenly be confronted with a sense of physical frailty, or perhaps mortality. The healthy partner may be forced to view the loved one in a different way, and may experience unfamiliar feelings of disbelief, sadness, and fear of the future. Changes are inevitable, and how couples respond to those changes depends on a universe of factors that will be explored in this book.

About this Book

While the topic of couples and illness is a difficult one, this book will not be depressing. The couples we interviewed spoke about loss, but they also described achieving levels of connectedness that would not have been possible within the normal routines of their pre-illness existence. And while some situations end with separation or the passing of the partner, others end with recovery, and many result in healing in ways that stretch far beyond the physical.

This is not a traditional self-help book. The situations encountered by couples living with illness don't lend themselves to simple answers. While you will find practical advice and tips, our emphasis is on portraying the effect of illness on the couple relationship through stories and the guidance of experts. Our couples candidly described the impact of illness on their roles, their communication, their connections, and their disconnections. They spoke openly about *what* they experienced and, perhaps more importantly, about *how* they solved problems and moved through difficult moments. Our couples talked about many intimate topics, including sex, money, assisted suicide, family strife, and more.

The population of people over sixty-five years old is expected to double in the coming decades. They are expected to live longer and to suffer increasingly debilitating and chronic diseases. Baby boomers will swell the ranks of the elderly, and many will live beyond the age of eighty-three. A longer life, unfortunately, can also mean more years of potential illness. This affects not only the ill person and the partner, but also health care providers, friends, and extended family members. This book will provide those who work with couples and illness—doctors, nurses, rehabilitation specialists, hospice workers, psychotherapists, spiritual caregivers, and other health care professionals—with a deeper understanding of the couple's experience of illness, along with more options for intervening in healing ways. If you are a friend or family member of a couple who is living with illness, it can be difficult to know how to relate to them and what to say. This book will prepare you to interact with the couple in ways that can be helpful for them and for you.

The world of couples living with illness is a cloistered one. The couple is isolated from support systems and unfamiliar with the new rules of engagement. New characters—doctors and other health care providers—enter and leave according to their own procedures and timetables. The couple is so immersed in an alien and frightening reality that they can't see over the wall to learn how other couples, each one in its own cloister, cope with similar challenges. This book knocks down the walls and makes visible, to the couple and to the people who care for them, the hardships and the solutions, the heartaches and the hopes.

Lessons from Real-Life Stories and Experts

In this book, you will read real-life stories of couples who have faced and become transformed by illness. Many of them crashed into heartbreaking choices: together or apart? Despair or hope? Home care or institution? Each couple found their own way to bear the insufferable—whether in community or in silence, exploring or denying, working through their crisis together or separately. In addition, experts share their knowledge about the effects of illness on intimacy, communication, family dynamics, and emotional connections, as well as on such practicalities as finances, dealing with the medical system, long-term care, and financial planning.

In this confusing array of choices, there is only one truth: No single approach is right for every couple. Each couple responds to illness in a personal way. The choices couples make are informed by a convergence of unique influences: their past experiences with illness, their community and its social mores, personal values, emotional and psychological makeup, finances, the support resources available to them, the health care system they depend on, family legacies, and their life together as a couple. A young couple still in the rosy discovery stage of their relationship may process illness differently than an older couple whose relationship has already weathered many upheavals. Demographics alone can never determine who will sink and who will rally. In fact, one couple's surrender may be equivalent to another's greatest act of courage.

By learning from the stories of our couples and hearing the advice of experts, you will see over the cloister wall that typically isolates couples living with illness, and you will find many insights that you can use to improve your own situation.

Why We Wrote this Book

As authors, each of us was drawn to this topic through our own experiences of devastating illness and its effect on our relationships. We were both disabled by our physical calamities and unsure of when—or if—we would ever recover. Our partners had complex choices to make about the nature of their commitment to us and the extent of their obligations as caretakers.

Each of us had to navigate the frightening territory of medical uncertainty, while mourning a traumatic blow to our relationships. We lived with pain, with the anguish of losing a relatively predictable future, with dependency on our partners, and with midnight aloneness. We discovered the depths of our own resilience, how much we were loved and could love, and how our quest for healing transformed our intimate relationships.

Each of us recovered, but not without years of hard work—repairing our bodies, reclaiming our identities as healthy women, and renewing our relationships. It became our mission to delve even deeper into the world of couples and illness, learn what we could from other travelers on this difficult path, and glean the advice of experts. We healed, and we want to express our gratitude by helping other couples faced with the trauma of illness or injury.

Many couples and surviving partners, generously and with courage, shared their stories with us. Their names and identifying data (including our own) have been disguised to protect their confidentiality. Many stories are composites that combine elements from several couples' experiences. Experts also freely shared their knowledge and insights. The experts we interviewed included psychotherapists, doctors, nurses, spiritual leaders, researchers, and more. Unless otherwise noted, all expert comments came from our interviews. Their thoughts are quoted within the chapters and also presented in sections separated from the main text by rows of dots.

What We Learned

Illness and trauma are always unwanted and often tragic. However, through writing this book, we've learned that it is possible to find your deepest and most abiding strength in suffering. We learned that, under extraordinary circumstances, people can rise to the extraordinary; that illness can be a gateway and not an epilogue; and that, even in the absence of a cure, healing is possible. As Hippocrates, the father of medicine, counseled, "A wise man should consider that health is the greatest of human blessings, and learn how by his own thought to derive benefit from his illnesses."

We also learned that hearing the stories of others and the counsel of trusted experts makes illness more bearable. Too often, couples facing illness find themselves standing alone, isolated from friends and family who are equally unnerved by the situation, and alienated by a health care system that speaks a foreign language and is already overburdened and under-resourced. People facing illness or trauma and the practitioners who help them have very useful stories and advice for weathering upheavals and for making decisions about preserving communication, finding the best specialists, managing managed care systems, researching alternative approaches, and creating supportive communities.

How this Book Works

In this book, we explore many of the questions that couples face when illness strikes. What happens at the intersection of love and obligation? How much should we do for those we love? How do we balance our own needs with those of our partner? How do we negotiate changing roles? How do we talk about difficult topics like fear, mortality, sex, anger, and separation? How do we deal with health care systems and legal issues?

Each chapter provides personal experiences and pragmatic recommendations from which you can extract the answers that apply to your own situation. If one of you is already sick, or if you are a friend or relative of the sick person, this book will be an essential guide. For those not yet in this position, we offer suggestions for beginning important conversations before illness strikes—on practical topics such as building a partnership with your doctor, health care proxies, and living wills; and on relationship-focused topics such as communication, intimacy, and hope. While nothing can eliminate the sorrow that illness delivers, preparing emotionally and practically for its arrival can strengthen your relationship and reduce some of the turbulence illness causes.

The Three Dimensions of Illness

When trapped in what feels like a maze, it helps to have a road map. The map will not eliminate the maze, but it can help you prepare for the next set of twists in the path. Through our interviews with couples and experts, we have observed that there are three dimensions to the maze of illness, and that each dimension consists of several patterns. Recognizing these dimensions can help you understand your current experience, consider the resources you need, and inject some order and direction into what can be a chaotic and overwhelming period. Although we have divided this book into sections that describe these three dimensions, it is important to recognize that they may not occur in strict sequence. You may have experiences that overlap or repeat themselves long after you thought they had been resolved.

Preceding the three dimensions is a period we call "the baseline." This is the pre-illness condition that has been your daily reality. It is rooted in what you have come to take for granted, with each partner owning a set of responsibilities. For example, one of you may handle all of the inner work of the household: the shopping, meal planning, cooking, and cleaning. The other may be in charge of the outdoor work: the garden, lawn, cars, house repairs. One of you might help children with homework and after-school activities, while the other reads bedtime stories. You have probably created a balance of intimacy and distance that suits you. This baseline period can be described as your "normal" life: family activities, work, getting together with friends, hobbies, and vacations. It may become the time you look back on with longing as you navigate the strange new geography of illness.

Your baseline "normal" state may end abruptly with an injury or a serious diagnosis, or it may become slowly transformed with the inexorable decline of a medical condition. Before you realize it, life has dramatically changed. However it happens, the Three Dimensions of Illness become your new reality as a couple.

The First Dimension: Crisis

A health crisis can arrive in many different ways. It may be precipitated by a catastrophic event, such as an injury, accident, or a serious diagnosis. It may arrive with the final shredding of the cover of denial that camouflaged a multitude of disconnected signs of illness. It may be the result of a sudden decline in an existing condition.

No matter how the crisis arrives, it is usually accompanied by fear and confusion. These emotions—along with a desperate yearning for reassurance—can easily displace sound judgment, so it is important to seek advice from medical professionals and perhaps psychological or spiritual counselors for help with important decisions made during this period. The shock of the crisis may persist for days or weeks or months. It is a frightening period of feeling off-balance, as if your world has fallen off its axis. You feel chaotic and lost, and search desperately for somewhere solid to plant your feet. The chapters in this section are about the moment the crisis first hits, and its immediate impact on the roles each partner plays.

The Second Dimension: Balancing Act

After the feeling of crisis subsides, you realize that a third party has entered your relationship: an ongoing health problem. This unwelcome guest is a demanding one and its needs often take precedence over your needs as a couple. This is a time of new learning, adjustment, and change as you try to regain your balance and reclaim your life.

During the Second Dimension, the demands of illness dictate a shift in the balance of responsibilities, which creates upheaval in routines and roles. This upheaval can raise profound questions about your dynamic as a couple. The well partner now finds the role of caretaker added to his or her roster of previous responsibilities, while the ill partner may feel inadequate because of an inability to function as before. You begin to see each other differently, and resentment or anger may build, mixed with unspeakable fear about the future. Some well partners have described feelings of anger toward their ill partners, accompanied by guilt and the need to suppress these emotions because, of course, the illness is no one's fault. Some ill partners describe a deep sense of guilt for burdening their healthy partner and forcing the relationship to adapt to the requirements of illness. Some partners may feel renewed appreciation for one another. Some couples are adept at weathering these changes; others feel swamped. Chapters in this section focus on communication, living together or apart, and active coping.

The Third Dimension: Regaining Equilibrium

At some point the situation will settle. Information has been gathered, advice received, and adjustments made. It will never, of course, be the same as the former baseline period, because the health crisis has changed the relationship forever. But a new normal has begun to emerge from the chaos.

For some couples, this new normal arrives with the death of one partner. For others, there is recovery. For still others, aspects of the illness or injury will become permanent. In every case, new ways of living must be created, and the story of the illness or injury becomes part of the history of the couple. Rebuilding the relationship can result in the discovery of a vibrant, reanimated spirit amidst a community of deepened friendships. However, some partners may feel ongoing isolation and depression. For everyone, regaining equilibrium is not a one-time event but a continuous passage. The chapters in this section explore grief and loss, discovering hope, intimacy and sexuality, and the practicalities of living with illness—such as financial planning, legalities, rehabilitation, and alternative health care.

Whether you are a couple at the epicenter of a crisis, coping with long-term chronic illness, or just beginning a discussion with your partner about personal preferences and plans in the event of illness, it can be helpful to have experienced voices offering guidance. Our goal is to equip you with strategies and tools for living with illness and for making choices that are right for you and your partner. This book will provide guidance that will make your path less solitary and more hopeful. You will know that you are not alone.

Part I
The First Dimension

Crisis

Chapter 1

The Moment: When Calamity Strikes

Couples drift from moment to moment, sometimes embracing, sometimes accusing. They count on the illusion of control while ignoring the ubiquity of chaos, the better to chart their lives with a sense of continuity and security. We like to feel we have it all figured out: when we will buy our first home; when the first baby will arrive, then the second. We plan on satisfying careers, traveling, growing old with dignity, and retiring with secure income streams. In fact some of us may separate or divorce, endure boring jobs, and wind up with cats instead of kids. But that is never the script we write for ourselves. And nowhere in our story is there a placeholder for the intrusion of illness.

Sudden trauma or a terrible diagnosis slams into us like a stray bullet. It penetrates our core in an instant, in the space between two breaths. The breath before was taken in the clear air of our old life. The breath after is caustic. It fades our dreams. It shoves our idealized images of our partner off their pedestals and immerses us in the reality of our own fragility. The patient is not the only casualty. Illness also attacks our belief in the future and in the promise of love.

In this chapter we meet two couples. Consuela and Mark had their former life ended by a sudden trauma. Linda and Frank's world changed suddenly through an unexpected complication of a planned surgical procedure. Both couples were thrown into crisis. Both found their way through what Consuela called the "dark tunnel" of illness.

Consuela and Mark: The Dark Tunnel

We sat with Consuela in the small den attached to the kitchen of her harborfront Victorian home. Thin, dark-haired, dressed in a soft brown shift, Consuela sat very still and spoke in a steady, quiet voice, as if the story she were about to tell required all her energy.

Consuela and Mark met in 1968. Mark was an adventurer who had organized workers in Yugoslavia and studied with renowned psychologist Jean Piaget in Paris. He had sailed oceans, skied mountains, and devoted himself to social justice. At the university where he was a professor, he was known as an iconoclast who fought for the rights of the marginalized.

Consuela grew up in Argentina, where she had briefly been married to a lawyer. She ended that relationship when he chose to pursue money, as she no longer wanted the uptown life. When a mutual friend introduced her to Mark, their immediate chemistry was heightened by a shared drive to find a purpose not rooted in material excess. They spent the first several years of their marriage traveling the world, then settled down after their second child was born.

The early glow of romance and world travel weakened under the daily realities of babies, housework, and Mark's academic life. Consuela chafed under the inequality that seeped into their relationship. Mark was older, more experienced, more financially secure, and free to enjoy the inspirational role he played with his students. Consuela was not only at home with their children and the chores, but she also felt isolated in their white, conservative, suburban community.

She decided to go to law school to garner more tools for her social justice efforts. This choice propelled a healthy shift in the balance of their relationship. Mark became more involved with the children and pitched in at home. Consuela began to feel more like an equal partner with her own base of expertise, income, and clout.

Mark and Consuela had weathered this realignment in their family life, one that might have swamped another couple. Their work, their relationship, and their family were evolving toward greater cohesiveness and reciprocity.

When Mark was sixty-five, his squash buddy, Spike, called Consuela one day to say that Mark, who played squash with the same fervor he engaged in all activities, had hit his head against the concrete wall while going after a shot. Unable to move his legs, Mark was in an ambulance on his way to the hospital. That night, a doctor said to Consuela, "Mark suffered an incomplete spinal cord injury that leaves him largely paralyzed. It is highly unlikely that he will ever recover." The bluntness of the doctor's pronouncement felt particularly harsh to Consuela since she did not know this doctor, and he had no knowledge of Mark's indomitable spirit.

The outer world faded as Consuela felt her blood pounding throughout her body. It was as if she had heard that Mark had already died. She was crushed beneath the weight of her own questions: What will we do? What will our lives be like? What will this devastation do to the man I love? "It was like I was driving frantically through a dark tunnel," she said, "whose only outlet was a black hole."

When Illness Arrives

When illness or trauma arrives, it does not land on a blank slate. It comes to rest on the emotional topography that has become your relationship. Its impact is shaped by the patterns and habits that govern your unique style of connecting to one another. Couples who are practiced at having difficult conversations under stressful circumstances have learned that it is the murky unspoken, not the sharp truth (when spoken with compassion), that may cause great damage to a relationship. Practicing this kind of communication prepares them well for the difficult conversations that illness requires. Couples who sacrificed their own intimacy to raise children or to pursue a career will find that illness often unearths the long-buried skeletons in their relationship.

· · · · · · · · · · ·

DR. ABBY CAPLIN — GHOSTS IN THE ROOM

Those who come to their relationship with a family legacy of caretaking and nurturance will experience illness differently from those whose families ignored or abandoned the ailing during times of misfortune. Abby Caplin, M.D., M.A., who has dealt with illness as family member, patient, physician, and counselor, says, "Whenever I see a couple, I assume there are at least six people in the room, not two. There is of course the couple, but standing behind each of them I see the images of their parents and, through them, the previous generations' reactions to illness and family crises."

. . . .

In addition to bringing these family ghosts into the sick room, each member of the couple also carries his or her own ennobling or unfavorable fantasies about the partner and the relationship. With illness, the familiar ground suddenly shifts. The partner who was always seen by his beloved as vigorous and reliable (whether he was or not) now appears gray and diminished by disease. The beloved who can't tolerate this change may berate the patient and minimize his complaints, or exaggerate her own inabilities in the hope that her now ill partner will magically recover and once again take over his accustomed responsibilities. A couple who modeled themselves on the embittered roles their parents played for decades and whose own intensity burned brightest in battle may find themselves unable to connect when illness deprives one of them of the gusto to keep fighting. You can end up holding so tightly to the old image that in order to sustain the illusion you reject the reality of the illness and, in so doing, reject your partner.

. . . .

DR. PIERRE FAUBERT — THE INITIAL ATTRACTION REMEMBERED

"When catastrophe strikes, the idealized images that couples have of their partners may shatter along with their physical health," says Jungian psychologist and ethicist Dr. Pierre Faubert, from his office in Montreal. "Either on their own or with professional help, it is often useful for couples to become consciously aware of why they were attracted to each other in the first place, and to recognize the transformation on their perceptions that illness brings."

. . . .

Consuela's and Mark's First "Moments"

Consuela and Mark's relationship was solid. They had adventured together, felt a steadfast love for each other, and had worked together to adapt their relationship to changing circumstances and needs. They had a sturdy emotional platform. They also had useful professional skills. Mark had spent his life as an activist for the disabled, and now was living as a person with severe disabilities. Even though his body had limited capacity, while still hospitalized he marshaled his mind and his passion to continue his advocacy work, on his own behalf and that of other patients. Consuela's legal work with the Department of Social Services gave her many of the tools she needed to manage the health care system and make the necessary arrangements to care for Mark at home.

However, even with such a stable base, the world they had so lovingly crafted, along with the egalitarian roles they had consciously refined, were extinguished in an instant. Formerly Mark's comrade, Consuela became his unflagging attendant. The mindfulness she had previously dedicated to her family's and her community's welfare contracted and locked on the slightest shifts in Mark's demeanor. She awoke with him at least four times a night when he needed pain medication. When he wet himself and the bed, she maneuvered his bulk into the shower room to bathe him, and then she changed the bedding. She then tried to submerge that muddled combination of exhaustion and frenzy that primary caretakers know all too well in a few remaining hours of sleep before she had to go to work.

Finding Your Way in the Darkness

When illness strikes, it inevitably becomes the hub around which your life revolves, and your activities are tethered to its mighty pull. Illness determines how far from home you can venture, whether you can continue to work, if you can eat the foods you enjoy, and whether and how you can be intimate with your lover. Partner becomes patient and, as if he were wearing a carnival mask, all you start to see on his once-familiar face is the somber profile of disease. Illness is a demanding taskmaster. As exhaustion sets in, resentment can supplant compassion, and passion and humor can vanish. It is possible to emerge from this dark tunnel and recover some of the sweetness of love by separating idealized image from reality and damaged body from person.

············

DR. PIERRE FAUBERT — THE POWER OF SILENCE

To truly find each other within the anarchy of illness, Dr. Faubert suggests that, for a moment, couples sit in silence. "Silence," he explains, "is the ultimate communion." When the turbulence of activity slows to stillness, and space is emptied of the words you hurl at your fears, you are left facing each other without filters. In silence you may be able to fathom that unique essence in your partner and in yourself where your commitment is sheltered. You may find that the image of the good or bad parent you had superimposed over your partner fades as you sit in communion, allowing the true self to emerge. And you may see that underneath the spoils of illness and the vandalism of the body, in the soul's marrow, there is something fundamental that persists and loves. When you are afraid, the hardest thing to do may be to sit in silence. But it is in this silence that you may discover the abiding aspect of self that can lift you above fear, hopefully to a place of healing.

•••

DR. PIERRE FAUBERT — A WISE GUIDE

Dr. Faubert recommends that the couple find a "wise person," a guide or a therapist who can accompany them to "a holding place, a sanctuary, a place of transcendence where the couple can experience silence and go through the pain to unveil the purer self." The fewer defenses you have up, the more fully this pure self can emerge, and the more you can experience love. "Love is a source of healing," Dr. Faubert says. "Love brings to being that which is not; love creates." If there is an awareness of love in illness, the couple, rather than coexisting and awaiting the appearance of the next symptom, can constantly create their reality and not be defined by exterior circumstances. Dr. Faubert suggests, "Illness can be the jolt that can remove the dullness from our lives, unveil the potential. It can help us concentrate our focus rather than being distracted by the noise. We can find direction when the noise is silenced, and we can hear the deep, profound voice within."

· · · · · · · · · · ·

Consuela's Path

Towards the end of our interview, Consuela looked out over the harbor. Her brown eyes held a spectrum of emotions: grief contained, serenity emerging, and new hopes pending. She reflected on her years with Mark. "After his injury, everything changed. I took on more, especially those responsibilities that had been his, while he retreated and found it hard to fully engage in any moment." It took time for Mark to redefine himself and for Consuela to adjust to the magnitude of the change.

Mark and Consuela rebuilt their lives together after his injury, as they had in the past. They renovated their house to make it handicap accessible. They moved their bedroom and his office to the first floor. They widened doorways and got rid of carpets so that his wheelchair could move more easily. In addition to making these physical changes, their roles completely shifted. Consuela became the interface with the outside world. She took on the financial, medical, and housekeeping functions. She also played a large part in Mark's personal care. Mark refocused on other areas. He re-established his relationship with his university and continued to do research and meet with students. Over time, though Mark never regained his mobility, he did find ways to become more active. With the help of attendants, an assist dog, and other adaptive devices, he was able to resume activities he loved: teaching, skiing, and sailing.

When Mark died seven years after his accident, Consuela, with great sadness, realized that if they had been granted more time, they might have reclaimed even more of their old relationship. She mourned his death deeply, and as painful as that was, she was gratified that at least she could feel love and know how truly she had been loved. With the help of her children and her community, over time, she was able to restore her place in the world and reclaim the happier memories of their marriage.

Linda and Frank: The Fork in the Road

There came a moment when Linda realized with dreadful clarity that she was alone in the body that had betrayed her. Even though her husband, Frank, was by her side, he could not inhabit her skin. The skin that separated them enclosed her in an impenetrable shell of isolation and affliction. Linda somehow knew that only she had the power to open the shell and emerge healed.

Linda was forty-three when she underwent surgery for a congenital heart defect. When she awoke, she slowly began to inventory her mind, senses, and body parts to see how well they still worked. When she got to her extremities, she realized that she could not move her left leg or her left arm. It was as if, during the operation, someone else's limbs had been sutured onto her body with no connection to her brain. A few days later, when movement still had not returned, her doctors informed her that while the heart procedure was a success, she had suffered a stroke, and there was no way to tell when—or if—she would recover her mobility. A program of physical and occupational therapy and a life of adaptation were the only approaches they could offer.

In an instant, Linda's joy at the successful outcome of her heart surgery evaporated, and her body clenched around a swelling sense of panic and despair. Her doctor's words, "We can't tell you if you will get better," carried the clout of prophecy. She envisioned a barren life, emptied of the ability to work as a writer, to play the cello, to drive, to hug her children.

Linda lay in her hospital bed, her hazel eyes focusing on the sliver of blue sky she could see through the window curtains, fiercely trying to will her left side to move. She became increasingly aware that she was stranded in her frozen body and that no matter how much Frank loved her, he was on the outside. His desire to make the trauma vanish only emphasized his powerlessness and increased her sense of aloneness. She suffered a double defeat: the ability to move unimpeded and her belief that the love she and her husband shared had created an indelible union of mind and body. Now her body had veered off down a grim path that Frank could not follow and that she could not escape.

"I had no time to adjust or consider choices," Linda said. "One day I'm fine, and the next day I'm told that I may be an invalid for the rest of my life." Within the turbulence of her despair, Linda knew with the elemental certainty that can appear at life's most merciless (and sublime) junctures that she could not accept this doctor's judgment. She remained in a shocked state for two weeks, then began working with her occupational and physical therapists, and slowly started to reclaim her authority over her own life.

One afternoon, Linda had a vision that was as clear to her as a billboard sign. She saw a fork in the road, two diverging avenues, and knew that she had to make a decision that would influence the course of her life. One direction led to giving up, to "despair and immobility." The signpost on the other road read, "Fight back." This road pointed to unknown terrain. She did not know what kind of fighting would be required or where the road would take her, but she knew she had to pick the "fight back" route. She began by turning away from doctors who offered her pessimism and actively sought out those who could be her partners in hope.

You Are Not a Statistic

Ironically, the surgeon who repaired her heart also left her heartbroken. While he and the neurologists may have considered it their obligation to present what they envisioned as the truth, they assumed too much. Statistical medical probabilities based on aggregate data don't necessarily apply to an individual, who is unique and has her own potentially miraculous capacities. Statistics can't take into account one patient's willpower, another's deep faith, and another's reliance on non-conventional healing. They also don't take into account the enormous value of a loving partner. Yet these factors, along with many others, can sometimes overturn the sentence of even a severe diagnosis.

With the initial shock of diagnosis, the injured person and the partner are extremely vulnerable. They feel as if they have been deposited on an alien planet where the laws of familiar physics no longer apply and the air is toxic. The suddenness of the change means there is a lag time between the new reality and their ability to function within it. All their normal coping skills remain on planet Earth even as they have to immediately learn to breathe in this new atmosphere. In this unhinged state, they naturally seek a powerful guide, and typically grant omniscient status to the doctor.

The doctor becomes the orientation point in this new and frightening universe.

Her words signify more than educated opinion; they become oracular. It is as if she can foresee their future and has the potential to return them to safe ground. Linda's heart surgeon's parting words were, "Sorry you stroked, but heart-wise you're fine." He was satisfied that he had done his job. Anything outside the surgical realm was not his responsibility.

"I felt that he had dismissed me as a whole person," said Linda. "I was just another surgical case to him." Had Linda not possessed some abiding source of internal steel, the surgeon's words might have become her living epitaph.

It is not unusual, in the aftershock of diagnosis, for patients and their partners to either submit silently to the sentence or pummel the doctor with questions as they desperately seek loopholes through which they can squeeze their fading hopes. The doctor remains the focal point. Her words at this delicate moment—where the mind is ricocheting from fear to fear, and the body and soul's natural healing abilities need encouragement—can have fateful impact.

In the initial shock of a serious diagnosis, patients have four fears: death, disability, pain, and abandonment. These fears are a mobius strip of moving, intertwined, recurring emotions and assumptions, which offer the doctor many opportunities to counsel and comfort. Gene Lindsey, M.D., president and CEO of Atrius Health/Harvard Vanguard Medical Associates, said, "There are ways in which doctors can present the patient's situation that are accurate without being callous, and can even be nourishing." He described his role as a "travel agent," guiding patients from where they are to where they need to be, making resources available to them along the way.

Doctor as Healer

During the initial crisis period, a time of panicked vulnerability and dependency, when your investment in your doctor's heroism is at its peak, it can be very hard to acknowledge the signs of a broken doctor-patient connection—or even to know what a healing, and not merely a medical, relationship looks like. In a healing context, your doctor can simply and repeatedly reassure you that he cares about you and will do his best to help you. He can inform you that there are many options for managing pain and disability, and that he will keep working to make you comfortable and help you improve.

A healing doctor can call on his own humility and acknowledge that while death or disability are possible, he can't write your next chapters or know the exact trajectory of your illness. Healing is being present and promoting hope while presenting the medical perspective, and, at the same time, acknowledging the patient's fears with compassion.

A doctor who understands healing will also acknowledge the well partner and recognize that person's pain. A couple can rejuvenate or injure one another, and when one is sick, both need help. If the well person falls apart or shuts down, both may wind up stranded.

One day, Frank allowed his eyes to well up with tears in the hallway outside Linda's hospital room, where he could be sure that his wife would not see him. One of Linda's doctors noticed him and said, "Oh, no! You need to be strong for her." Frank was surprised and frustrated that a physician would not recognize the validity of his emotions. He had spent the past three days sitting in a chair by Linda's bed, watching her paralysis and panic, and experiencing his own fear. He did not need to be told to be strong. He was being Herculean.

Frank said, "If only the doctor had said, 'I know this must be hard for you, too.' That would have helped me feel less alone." Instead, this doctor provided no support and left him carrying his wife's desperation and his own misery in silence.

A doctor who is a true healer becomes a guardian of hope for both partners. He understands that even when the body is failing and despair is rising, hope can still be found. A psychologist who suffers from a neurological disorder and has been at the doorstep of health crises herself explains the persistence of hope in this way:

"There is always something to be hopeful about, no matter what condition you're in. When you have health, you can be hopeful about having any of your dreams come true. Once your body fails you, you can rest your hope in your emotions. You can hope that you will still feel love and compassion for others, and for yourself. If your emotions become emptied, you still have your spirit, and you can hope to connect to something greater than yourself, something that has a light to shine on your shadows. And when the spirit is gone, then you have already become something else, and who knows what hopes await you there."

If you and your partner ever feel that your doctor is not providing you with the support and guidance you need, it is time to either transform the relationship with your existing doctor or, if that is not possible, to look for another doctor. Luckily, Linda's primary care doctor, who became her companion throughout her ordeal, never abandoned her or hope for her recovery. He kept reminding her, "The body can heal. That is what it is programmed to do."

Finding Equilibrium

There are ways in which you and your partner can regain control of the after-diagnosis upheaval. You can be strong working as a team instead of isolating yourselves behind masks of stoicism. You can hold hands, face the doctor together and help one another ask questions and explore the implications of your new situation. You can divide up tasks such as Internet research on the illness, finding specialists, and dealing with insurance claims.

You can also make a conscious effort to counterbalance one another emotionally so that when one is frightened, the other can comfort. In this way, the healthy partner does not wind up locked into the role of perpetual cheerleader, and the ill person does not have to wear the mask of the clown who cries inside.

Another Fork in the Road

Linda's husband, Frank, had his own fork in the road to navigate. During Linda's week-long hospital stay, Frank—though he, too, was frightened—saw his job as being the "good husband," at her side at all times, putting her needs first. "It never occurred to me to do anything else," he said.

After Linda returned home, he realized that this was not going to be a short-term illness, and he began to consider his role in their changed circumstances. He knew that her stroke would change their situation, but he didn't want it to define their relationship. He wanted normalcy to continue as far as possible in their own lives, and those of their two young children. Linda needed lots of practical, daily help—with showering, toileting, dressing, and eating. Frank decided to spend his time meeting Linda's emotional needs rather than her physical ones. He was not going to become her caretaker. He would remain her husband and safeguard their adult dialogue and intimacy.

Initially, Linda did not understand, and was upset by what she perceived as Frank's disengagement. All she knew was that she needed assistance and that he wasn't helping. She became angry at Frank for what she experienced as his unreasonable refusal to help.

Fortunately, their insurance paid for home health aides to assist Linda with daily activities, while Linda dedicated all her energy to getting better. She performed the exercise routines prescribed by her physical and her occupational therapists for hours every day. She ate well and rested whenever she needed to. Frustrated with the limitations of conventional Western medical regimens, Linda used her background as a science and medical writer to become an integrative health specialist and incorporated meditation, yoga, the Alexander technique, and craniosacral therapy into her repertoire. Frank rejoiced in her every new accomplishment. Within a year, she had fully recovered, with only a slight weakness in her left hand remaining.

Ultimately, Linda was glad Frank had chosen his own fork in the road. "As much as I hate to admit it, he was right. He preserved the essence of the 'us' that was most important. He protected my dignity and my privacy. He remained my husband, never my nurse. Neither of us had to carry the legacy of a patient-caretaker relationship into my recovery. This was very important, especially in the context of our romantic relationship."

Reconsecrating the Relationship through the Crucible of Illness

Ester R. Shapiro, Ph.D., psychologist, researcher, professor, and author of *Grief as a Family Process: A Developmental Approach to Clinical Practice*, focuses her work on the ways in which people and their families deal with extraordinary life challenges, including illness and death. In situations of illness, she emphasizes the need to avoid "medicalizing" everything and to develop "positive coping," a focus on accomplishments, goals, and problem-solving.

. . . .

DR. ESTER SHAPIRO — NOT ALONE IN THE DARK

Dr. Shapiro reminds us that "illness enters at a particular moment in the lifecycle and the ecology of a couple and impacts the couple's way of accomplishing their goals. Behind the couple is a whole lifetime of experience against which the experience of the moment registers. Illness lands squarely on the bond the couple has established, onto their family situation, onto their history of negotiating prior troubles, and onto their stage of life. Illness drops into this entire constellation."

In order for a couple to share the trauma of illness rather than be split by it, Dr. Shapiro recommends that they develop a shared view of the illness and that they see it as "something you climb, another challenge to deal with," rather than as an ending. Just as Dr. Faubert suggests sitting in silence to make contact with what is essential, Dr. Shapiro advises reflecting on the insights illness might reveal.

Illness compresses time and summons mortality and can help us filter out the trivial. Paradoxically and surprisingly, the darkness illness casts can illuminate the sparkle of the transcendent that everyday normalcy eclipses. We can attend to what is truly important with intention and can live each moment potentially feeling "more alive with illness than the deadness of life before illness," says Dr. Shapiro.

Dr. Shapiro recognizes that positive coping can be particularly difficult if the couple is overwhelmed by their situation and the crushing burdens of job loss, inadequate insurance coverage, and diminished functionality. But ameliorating the stresses comes from "feeling you're not alone and understanding your mission both as a couple and as individuals." Dr. Shapiro believes it is possible for the couple to achieve a heightened state of connection during this distressing time by "reconsecrating the relationship through the crucible of illness and using the situation to discover what you truly love and what values you want to live by." To reconsecrate, to rebuild a deeper, more profound connection, she asks couples to consider the following questions:

- What are you trying to accomplish?

- What barriers are in the way?

- What strengths can you call on?

- What might you be dragging along from your family of origin that is no longer helpful?

In essence, she counsels couples to "love each other, support each other, and don't leave each other alone in the dark."

. . . .

Balancing Mutuality and Autonomy

Linda's and Frank's crucible did make them stronger as a couple. Linda took charge of her recovery, and that self-empowerment spilled over into other areas of their relationship. She grew more independent and resilient. The confidence she earned by her victory in the arena of illness also increased her confidence as a writer. Witnessing Linda's determination, ingenuity, and self-sufficiency, Frank felt freer to explore those activities that offered him respite and pleasure that were separate from her. He reclaimed his athleticism, undertook long, difficult bike rides, and grew increasingly fulfilled by seeing the obstacles he was capable of surmounting.

Both Frank and Linda took personal responsibility for overcoming their separate challenges, while at the same time they continually "reconsecrated" their relationship. Finding this balance between mutuality and autonomy during a severe illness experience prepared Frank and Linda well to achieve rewarding levels of growth—individually and as a couple.

Postscript

When serious illness or trauma threatens the myth of immortality, a myth we use to bind our anxieties and shield us from our own fragility, our lives change forever. The moment that this myth is shattered, and in the days to come, our current realities and our assumptions about future possibilities become undone and redone in ways we never imagined in our pre-illness lives. This quantum upheaval lands smack on the couple relationship and that connection gets sorely tested. Its strengths and its weaknesses reveal themselves as the couple negotiates both the tangles of the health care system and the labyrinth of their own love.

For the partners to find one another, rely on one another, and connect with the heart of their relationship, they must pay close attention. The onslaught of fear and the invasion of the medical system need to be managed so that they don't obliterate the couple's power. For that power to serve the couple in this time of crisis, the partners need to stop, to see one another, to plan together, and to remember who they are as a couple.

Illness can indeed be the crucible in which the couple recreates their relationship and discovers new possibilities for greater intimacy and connection. Dr. Faubert reminded us that "illness can be the jolt that removes the dullness from our lives." Dr. Shapiro affirmed that "we can be more alive with illness than with the deadness of life before illness." However, the "moment," the initial crisis phase of illness, is choked with doctors, specialists, tests, procedures, and fears that threaten to overwhelm the couple's equilibrium. How can a couple prevent the initial upheaval of illness from swamping them?

Here are some possibilities:

- Remember and talk about what brought you together in the first place. Limitations and anxiety can easily dominate. Talk about what you admire in one another. Be purposeful in remembering strengths.

- Set aside time to engage in the familiar activities (that are still possible) that bring you together in a few moments of calmness, and even happiness.

- Try to separate the person from the illness. The illness may alter the partner's abilities and require adaptations, but the essence of that person persists and can be reached. Many people with cancer have said, "I may have cancer, but cancer doesn't have me." The self is not the illness. The illness only knows biology; the self contains multitudes.

- Sit together in silence. This is one of the most powerful interventions a couple can do, and potentially a difficult one. If you sit in silence together long enough, the air clears and activity and anxiety are subdued by the stillness. In that stillness, you may find a place where love and strength persist and can refuel the relationship.

- While the well partner will most likely wind up in some form of helping role, the couple should do what they can so that the entirety of the couple relationship does not become one of caregiver and patient.

- Divide up tasks. Some may be too demanding for the ill partner, but there will be others he or she can handle—e.g. Internet research, making appointments, keeping track of medications and symptoms. If the ill partner can, he should handle his daily care needs (showering, dressing, feeding). If not, consider using home health aides to preserve the couple relationship. (This can often be covered by insurance or provided for free by some community health centers.) And if he can attend to family needs (shopping, preparing meals, chauffeuring kids), he should do that, too. The ill partner should be encouraged to act to the limits of his ability.

- Be balanced about providing emotional support. One partner suffers the illness in his body, but two lives are dislocated. Two people are afraid, angry, and sad, and in need of clarity and support. If the partners can't bolster each other and make wise decisions together, often a psychotherapist or spiritual counselor can help.

Couples who are at the outset of their illness journey are unbalanced and naturally look to their doctor or to a specialist to guide them. Most often, they find wise counsel. Unfortunately, many doctors work in environments that are overextended and under-resourced, where the pressure to see patients in fifteen-minute intervals makes it hard to attend to the relationship and hope-building sides of patient care. Ill partners can do their part by coming to appointments prepared with their own research, with questions for the doctor, and with their well partner (or a friend or relative) who can listen and take notes.

Patients may also look to their doctor to help them find the hope in their situation. Even in desperate situations, some form of hope can be found. It may be important to seek doctors and specialists who know how to tell the truth without dampening hope. In fact, hope may be a crucial motivating and healing element. If you and your doctor are not well suited, first talk to her to see if clarifying assumptions can rectify the relationship; if that doesn't work, it may be time to find a new doctor.

Finally, it is important to remember that hope is always possible, and that hope is healing. Hope can be as important as medicine. Hope can be found not only in the quest for a physical recovery, but also in healing the partner relationship and in growing psychological maturity. As one partner said, "Your life may not be the same. But you can have a good life, even a better life together."

Chapter 2

Changing Roles:
Who Is Taking Care of Whom?

You and your loved one came to this relationship imprinted with the predisposi-
tions and personalities of generations of your family members filtered through
your own unique life experiences. Whether you are aware of it or not, you are the
product of a multi-generational pattern of relationships that influences how you relate
to your partner every day.

This pattern may be seen as a kind of "dance" that has clear parts. Its choreography dictates when you come together and when you break apart; how you deal with
intimacy and conflict, express your emotions, raise your children, and handle illness.
The patterns of movement contained in this dance lurk beneath the level of your conscious awareness and determine how you and your partner relate to each other. In one
couple, emotions may be seen as dangerous territory to be danced over as quickly as
possible. Another couple may only connect when fighting. Some couples meet illness
with silence and stoicism, others regress and manipulate, while others embrace one
another and their community.

In some families, male and female parts are rigidly defined: the man lifts the heavy
objects, and the woman orbits around him, sheltering him from the responsibilities
of child-rearing and housekeeping. In others, the male and female roles are fluid, with
each partner modulating behavior based on the needs of the situation. These movements are made even more complex by the fact that women are not only influenced
by other women in the family, nor are the men solely influenced by male role models.

We all contain male and female roles. Same-sex partners are also bequeathed male and female family behavior patterns.

In fact, often what attracts us to our partner initially is a quiet, unspoken intuition that this is the person with whom we can "dance." When couples fit well together, it is often because the choreography of their emotions and roles is well-synchronized. In everyday life, couples come to rely on the complementarity and predictability of each other's movements or roles in the relationship. One partner shops; the other cooks. One nurtures; the other negotiates. One starts a chore, the other finishes it. This equilibrium will persist with relative stability, usually until some life event forces a disruption. When one member of a couple becomes ill or incapacitated, this balance, and the unspoken rules that govern it, will change. Illness forces partners to learn to dance to an unfamiliar beat.

One cardiologist we spoke with told the story of a couple that had a "dysfunctionally functional" marriage for many years. The husband's sudden need for a heart valve replacement brought to the surface the wife's terrible experience with her father's death from congestive heart failure when she was a child. The cardiologist said, "Medical events bring marital issues to a head." The wife, because of her family history, was so disturbed by her husband's illness that she abandoned her role as nurturer of others and became depressed, then suicidal.

No couple is prepared for the magnitude of change brought on by serious illness. Typically, what was once a relationship of equals becomes one of caregiver and patient. How a couple negotiates changes in roles forced on them by illness can have a profound impact not only on the relationship but also on the course of the illness experience.

In this chapter, we meet two couples. Emily and Wayne, both in their fifties, bring abiding love but very different rhythms to their relationship. Their potential for sudden emotional eruptions forced them to communicate about their differences often and to learn to adapt to changing circumstances. They cultivated "relationship agility," so that when they were faced with a devastating illness, they had the tools they needed to cope. The second couple, Paul and Mary, both in their seventies, kept to more traditional role definitions. Paul dealt with the world. Mary dealt with the family. They loved deeply and smoothly. This equilibrium served them well until illness tilted their world.

Emily and Wayne: Equal but Different

Emily and Wayne were quick to love but slow to find a rhythm that could contain their differences. Emily, a therapist, is deeply introspective, psychologically minded, and adept at reading the subtitles underlying her interactions with Wayne. After a few months of dating, she could tell if something serious was on his mind by the way he exhaled. After a year, she was able to name and explain his emotions before he even recognized he was feeling something. And, much to Wayne's consternation, he realized that she was usually right.

Wayne is a scientist who absorbs the world in chunks of data and can synthesize large quantities of information. He is a problem-solver and can turn Emily's stray comments about her feelings into platforms for data analyses that lead to logical conclusions, which, much to Emily's annoyance, are often helpful.

Emily is a planner; Wayne is spontaneous. Emily likes neatness; Wayne leaves his clothes strewn about the house. Emily completes work projects weeks before deadline; Wayne needs that eleventh-hour pressure to finish. Emily likes to get to the airport an hour and a half before a flight; Wayne enjoys a frantic dash down the airport corridor, squeezing through the door seconds before the final boarding call. They coincided in their love for vigorous hiking.

How could these very different people have found the common ground on which to build love? They met in 1976, while in their twenties, on a blind date. They fell into "like," and with time and proximity, they fell in love. They dated steadily but did not marry until 1985. They did not have children.

After the initial romance faded and they settled into the routines of life together, they began fighting. Their differences became cloaks to hide under as well as stones to hurl at one another. Emily berated Wayne for his insensitivity to her needs. Wayne retreated into silence and appeared unreachable. This made Emily escalate her interrogation, which caused Wayne to become even more evasive. The cycles of this dance were self-perpetuating.

With the help of couples' therapy, they struggled to learn how to join together in a compassionate evaluation of the ways they grated on each other. To their surprise, they discovered that what each needed from the other and found lacking was exactly the area where the other needed to grow. Emily would cajole or torment Wayne to express his feelings. As Wayne learned the language of emotion, he found, to his delight, that a world of insight and imagination opened up to him. Wayne pushed Emily to become more spontaneous and often set up last-minute situations (inviting guests over or getting movie tickets) that left her little time to engage in her early-bird planning behaviors. As Emily learned that letting go in minor situations did not result in disintegration, she learned to become more playful and open to sensation in other areas of her life. Emily and Wayne said that in the crucible of their relationship, "We grew each other up."

"You can't change the illness, but you can fix the issues."

One day in late November, 1999, Emily began noticing the insidious signals of what she thought was yet another urinary tract infection. Over the past few years, as she drew nearer to her fiftieth birthday, she had become quite familiar with the sensation of afternoon bladder pressure, itchiness, and urinary urgency that started as a tickle, and by early evening could feel like a herd of stallions rampaging across her pelvis. As usual, she scheduled a urine culture and began taking antibiotics.

Surprisingly, this time the urine culture came back negative, yet the symptoms continued, undiminished by the first, then the second, course of medication. Over the next several weeks she experienced a dramatic increase in bladder pressure that was only temporarily relieved through urination.

Emily described her increasing pain as a "twelve on a one-to-ten scale, where ten means shoot me now." She said, "It was as if I had a giant closed fist inside my bladder, growing larger as it squeezed more tightly. As it grew, it pressed upward and outward, against all neighboring organs, until my whole pelvic cavity felt as if it were about to explode. There were times when I wouldn't have been surprised if some alien squid had come bursting out of my gut."

Emily, an active, empathic, thinking woman who was used to engaging mightily with the outside world, watched helplessly as her realm constricted to the single point she shared with her increasing pain. Instead of the dance of equals she was used to with Wayne, the only name on her dance card now was "pain." Every moment of every day was consumed with frightened, manic attempts to escape from pain's fierce grip.

She could no longer work, cook, or see her friends, and soon she could not leave the house. Wayne grew desperate as he was forced to witness his beloved cower and weep like a child tormented by an abusive parent. This was a problem Wayne could not solve and a dynamic that Emily could not psychoanalyze away. They were both thrown off balance, tumbling wildly, grasping at air. They no longer knew how to connect.

· · · · · · · · · · ·

DR. CAROL WOGRIN — FIXING THE ISSUES

"Couples have familiar patterns of communication and ways of maintaining some degree of emotional and psychological distance, even couples that are close," says Carol Wogrin, Psy.D., R.N., Director of the National Center for Death Education. "Partners become comfortable with this level of distance. Illness clogs up the system and forces the couple to deal with the issues that are upsetting their roles and degree of distance." Illness forces change, but the couple system automatically resists and strives to ignore or absorb the change into its customary routines. The resulting tension between illness forcing and the couple system resisting frays the strands that hold the couple together. If the couple doesn't address the radical upheaval illness delivers, their interactions can become toxic or empty. Dr. Wogrin describes a familiar illness scenario: "The ill woman responds to her situation with an escalation of emotion. The well man wants to fix it, but can't. He feels desperate and pulls away. She turns up the emotional volume. He backs away even further. The escalation continues." Dr. Wogrin concludes, "You can't change the illness, but you can fix the issues."

· · · · · · · · · · ·

Pain displaced Wayne as Emily's primary relationship. She could not afford to squander energy connecting with him. Every ounce was reserved for her battle with pain. Wayne could only watch and mechanically attend to the daily needs of their lives. Emily, the intuitive, and Wayne, the analyst, lost all standing in the presence of pain. The carefully crafted architecture of their relationship toppled.

To make matters worse, there seemed to be no relief in sight. Emily's primary care doctor was baffled but willing to refer the couple to specialists. Over the course of a year and a half, Emily saw a neurologist, an orthopedist, a gynecologist, a urologist, and even a uro-gynecologist. She was MRI'd and CAT scanned from her brain to her knees. She saw an acupuncturist, a chiropractor, a homoeopath, a polarity therapist, and an energy healer. They all said basically the same thing: "The good news is that we can find nothing terminal or broken enough to provoke this degree of pain. The bad news is we can find nothing..."

For over a year, Emily's pain raged on uncontrolled. There was a seven-month period during which she was not able to sit or lie down. Emily said, "When I sat it felt as if rigid, sharp sticks dug into every tender spot I had. When I lay down, it was as if any surface became hard granite that sent pain shooting up and down my body. In order to sleep, I assembled a ring of pillows on top of a lightly inflated air mattress on top of my usual bed. I gently lowered my body into the center of the circle so that the pillows supported the bulk of my weight and my back barely skimmed the mattress. However, nothing was soft enough, and it felt as if there were glass shards on every surface."

Balancing on the Edge

According to psychologist and researcher Suzanne McCarthy, Psy.D., who has studied couples and cancer, one of the most notable gender differences for couples dealing with illness is that women tend to have and rely on a wider support network of family and friends, while men do not readily seek support and tend to focus on practicalities. Wayne not only took over all household tasks, he spent endless hours slashing his way through the insurance jungle. He carried out Internet research to find the most current thinking about pain management, and cold-called researchers whose articles pointed in a hopeful direction to ask their advice. He was the couple's interface with the world. Emily, however, did not fit the profile Dr. McCarthy describes for women. She isolated herself completely and relied on Wayne as her sole support.

Illness had forced them to abandon their old patterns of relating and to choreograph new ones. Luckily, their history prepared them well to adapt to their differences and to changing circumstances. In the past, when their natures turned them momentarily into antagonists, they knew from their couples' therapy work how to hold hands and create a safe zone, an emotional incubator from which always emerged new and beautiful patterns for connecting. They knew not only how to reconfigure their roles; they also knew how to have difficult conversations and to say, "I want," "I can't," "I need you to," "I'm afraid," "I hate you," "I love you."

When Emily was momentarily able to peer through the darkness, she could see that her pain immobilized Wayne, causing depression. She struggled to find a way to reconnect and to create new roles for each of them that would have meaning in their current situation. Emily needed peace, not psychology, and Wayne needed to be active, not analytic. She began asking him to stroke her hair, rub her feet, read *Alice in Wonderland* aloud to her until she fell asleep—actions that calmed her fears and eased her body. Perhaps the most important task she requested of him was to hold the hope for her, since she could no longer find any inside herself. In these ways Emily could receive some comfort, and Wayne could be active and feel useful. The most essential gift she could offer was to recognize how loving and generous Wayne was being and how impossible this nightmare was for him, too. In her decimated state, she could at least continue to know him.

They also learned to communicate on a deeper and more authentic level than they had reached in their healthier past. When Wayne needed respite from watching Emily in pain, he was able to tell her, "I love you. My heart is breaking for you. If I could take your pain into my body, I would gladly do so. But for me to continue to be strong for you, I need some time away from your pain. Not you, your pain." Emily could say to Wayne, "I can't bear this another second. I wish I were dead," while Wayne just held her, both of them knowing that wishing for death is not the same as committing suicide and even served as a release valve for Emily's growing despair.

· · · · · · · · · · ·

Abby Caplin M.D., M.A., a physician and therapist who specializes in treating people with chronic illness, emphasizes the importance of "unconditional presence." Dr. Caplin says, "Just being present with a person who is ill, without trying to fix it, is the single most important thing a partner can do."

· · · · · · · · · · ·

Recovery and Recalibration

However, even with all their adaptive skills, neither Emily nor Wayne could tolerate for much longer the desecration that pain inflicted on their relationship. Emily's brother played basketball on a team composed of middle-aged men like him, with bad knees and strong financial portfolios. Many of these men were doctors. One of them tossed off a comment about a brilliant pain specialist in Emily's area whom he had heard speak at a conference. Emily waited three months for an appointment with this doctor. Her first visit with this pain specialist was the turning point she and her husband had been praying for.

Over the course of the next six months, the pain specialist worked assiduously to find the right medication cocktail to alleviate Emily's pain, even though a clear diagnosis remained elusive. He was a researcher and a clinician and could blend the most current pain relief investigations with first-hand experience with patients. This winning combination of scientist and practitioner roles gave him knowledge and empathy, and a rare ability to listen to the horror of Emily's story while conveying hope.

The cocktail began to work, and Emily started to re-enter the world. She went for walks, cooked dinner, groomed the dog, read books—activities that pain had stolen from her. After a few months, she even began to believe that she might get her life back and be able to work, travel, and be an adult partner to Wayne.

The transition to new normalcy was not as seamless as Emily and Wayne had expected. Wayne had grown accustomed to being the protector, the preeminent hunter-gatherer in the family. As burdensome as his role had been during Emily's illness, he had grown used to being in control of their affairs and was reluctant to change. During the illness, Emily had become accustomed to being dependent on Wayne to shelter her from material demands and emotional intrusions. She now felt inadequate handling complex demands. She turned to Wayne to deal with income tax forms, the broken furnace, driving beyond city limits, and meddlesome relatives. She wanted to have her independence and to be coddled. The result was an imbalanced relationship.

Again, Emily's and Wayne's fluency at discussing sharp-edged issues served them well when they needed to disentangle from roles that were no longer necessary. Each was able to name the pieces of their pain-infested lives that remained embedded in their current identities. Once they acknowledged these leftovers, they began to renegotiate more mature roles that gave them a solid balance between responsibility and comfort.

It took time, and some backsliding, but eventually, Emily and Wayne found their sweet spot. They had their love, which had never dimmed, and they had survived the fire. They were equal partners again; but added to the load each carried was a new gift they now shared. The gift, one that their traumatic experience of illness gave them, was a heightened awareness that each moment without pain, without illness, without the footprint of death, was the true joy. Moments of sadness or anger couldn't diminish that joy, nor could acquisitions or accomplishments compare with it.

Paul And Mary: 'Til Death Do Us Part

Paul and Mary's story, as told to us by their daughter, illustrates role changes that evolved more gradually. Their pattern is familiar: as the ill partner declines, the well one slowly assumes the role and responsibilities of the ill partner and carries more of the weight of the relationship. Paul and Mary's story, however, took a dramatic turn.

When his wife was diagnosed with Alzheimer's disease, Paul made the decision to care for her at home. Since both he and Mary were deeply committed to family, to personal integrity, and to each other, for Paul the choice was obvious. When his children questioned the wisdom of this decision, he explained, "We've been in love for fifty years. I promised to love her for better or worse. It's been great, and now it's worse. This isn't the time when I abandon her. This is my job now."

Paul had dedicated his life to fairness, service, and commitment. In the 1930s, he was a farm boy in New England, bound by the rhythms of land and livestock. He learned about acceptance from the fierce winter winds and the parched summer soil. He subjugated his needs to the schedule of cows waiting to be milked and chickens needing to be fed. He was a dutiful son to his indifferent father and a loving helper to his overextended mother.

At college he was class president and captain of the soccer team. He served his country in three wars. After his military career, he went to law school at age forty-two and came out an ardent prosecutor and guardian of victims' rights. At home with Mary and their five children he was the "Big Daddy"—protective, authoritative, at times commanding, at times nurturing, and always proud and loving.

Abandoned by her disinterested father at the age of four, Mary was raised in the 1930s by a humiliated teenage mother. Like Paul, she founded her life on commitments rooted in her earliest experiences. She was committed to her own intelligence and competency, to a vital life, and most urgently, to an indestructible family tethered by faith, love, and honor.

At college Mary was a diligent student, an energetic sorority sister, and was elected beauty queen of her class. After graduation, she went to an Ivy League university to study architecture and fulfill her dream of becoming a city planner. Instead, she dropped out after one year to marry Paul in 1954, and became an army wife and mother.

Paul and Mary were soul mates and treasured each other's company above all else. Paul was large, muscled, and commanding. Mary was shorter, slender, and sweet. Paul provided; Mary nested. He was Big Daddy to her, and she was home to him. These roles became fixed early in their relationship and continued harmoniously for many years. Even after five decades of army and legal service, and after fifty years of marriage, Paul remained unfailingly devoted to his wife, always greeting her with a kiss when he returned home from the office, and smiling when she entered the room.

The Slow Seep of Illness

In 1995, when Mary was in her late fifties, her husband and adult children began to notice subtle changes in her behavior that grew more pronounced with each passing month. She stopped eating and drank only Coca-Cola. Her beautiful face was lined with sadness, and she sighed, "What do I have to live for?" Paul's eyes teared as they lingered on her mismatched outfit and the cracker crumbs clinging to her shirtfront. He watched her float from room to room in the house, now vacated by their grown children, as if she were seeking sanctuary from enemies who were slowly stealing her memory.

Over the next seven years Mary declined steadily. She started keeping lists of years and the key events that occurred in each. She also kept lists of the names of her children and grandchildren. Eventually she forgot where she had placed her lists. She railed that no one listened to her or understood the word salad she had begun to speak. She sat for hours in an armchair, her eyes unfocused, her nails scratching the fabric as if trying to claw her way out of a locked room.

As time went on, the daily care tasks became more difficult. Paul helped Mary bathe, dress, eat, and even use the toilet. A few times he found the house empty and the front door open. He rushed outside, his legs and stamina weakened by diabetes, to find her standing on a street corner, looking like a lost child. He began to bring her with him to the office and to court. She sat in a chair, watching him with empty eyes, while he worked. His children worried about the strain on his health.

Alzheimer's, the Terrorist

Alzheimer's disease is a terrorist and a thief. It steals the mind and the soul slowly, toying with hope, breaking down resilience, and eventually forcing people to surrender. For years couples may notice the slow erosion of memory, recognition, and language, while also straining to ignore or explain away or at least postpone naming what is at the root of this dissipation of identity. Finally, the name is spoken and confirmed by specialists, and becomes the hub around which the couple revolves.

The promise of love's protection is revealed to be temporary. As the illness cuts deeper, the spoken or assumed vows partners made to each other get severed. They are equals no more. Partner roles are irredeemably demoted to parent-child, to care-giver-patient. Unlike other serious illnesses that savage the body but leave the mind available for connection, Alzheimer's takes mind and body. Warm, shared memories and fantasies of future possibilities dissolve. Only present connection remains, filled with endless emotional and physical chores for the well partner to carry out. Both partners suffer uncertainty, sadness, anger, and loneliness, broken by occasional tender touches, smiles, and sweet moments.

Eventually the choice that no one wants to confront forces itself on the couple in a seemingly endless stream of questions: Can the patient be safe at home? What level of home care is necessary and affordable? What role should you (and any of your adult children) take on? To what extent should you contort your current life to care for your loved one, who gave so much to make your life better? What do you do about any anger or resentment you feel about the past and present difficulties in your relationship? How much is too much? When should you consider a care facility? What constitutes good enough caretaking? How do you tell when caretaking crosses the line into self-destruction? What is loyalty and what is betrayal?

There is no checklist of right choices. The answers live in the core of our beings and may not be known until events force them to the surface. You may have had many frank discussions with your partner about aging and end-of-life wishes. At this moment, you rest with the confidence that when the time and circumstances come, as agreed, you will place your partner in a nursing home. But when that time does come, and you see that frightened confusion in her eyes as she reaches out with an unsteady hand to stroke your cheek, you realize you don't know what to do. Or you may have determined to take care of your partner no matter what—until that "what" slams you down with such force that you can barely stand. Your role as protector or nurturer spins wildly as it bumps up against all these questions.

These questions are layered with the full spectrum of emotions and values: love and anger, duty and resentment, selflessness and selfishness, pride and shame, and ultimately powerlessness in the face of circumstances that we can manage but never reverse. How can a couple begin to untangle all these issues? Dr. Gene Lindsey emphasized, "It is important to create the conversation." This requires "creating a place of safety where the couple can speak openly," advised Reverend John Buehrens, former president of the Unitarian Universalist Association and currently a Unitarian Universalist church minister. "Perhaps with a trusted advisor, the couple can set conditions for grace to unstick things."

Whether you believe in grace, the universe, or your own will, it is essential to prepare a "holding environment," a space in which partners reach out to each other with compassion and commit to discussing these difficult questions honestly. Pick a time when the ill partner is still alert. Pick a location that is safe and comfortable. Begin by agreeing that this discussion is above all a vehicle to promote well-being and carry you to the next level of connection, and it is therefore essential that the fears and sorrow emerge, along with the practicalities.

Once you have created this "safe space" and are ready to have the conversation, "Be as concrete as possible about the next step in circumstances that are uncertain," Dr. Lindsey advised. "The sands of illness shift unexpectedly, so it is hard to devise a long-term plan. But you can invent your way forward by making a plan based on the current status, while being alert to the need to alter that plan as circumstances change."

· · · · · · · · · · ·

DR. RUTH LIPMAN — STOP. THINK. THEN ACT.

Four important elements to consider when planning care:

1. How can the patient maintain as much independence as possible?

2. How can the patient be made as physically and emotionally comfortable as possible?

3. What information do you need to get to make wise decisions (about treatments, care facilities, home care options, end-of-life options)?

4. What resources do you have (financial, legal, community)?

Dr. Ruth Lipman, research associate with the Foundation for Informed Medical Decision Making, says that, "What you learned in kindergarten pretty much holds in terms of basic guidelines. Stop. Think. Then act." In other words, don't rush to action precipitously and possibly foolishly in the frenzy of the moment. "For people facing a health catastrophe," says Dr. Lipman, "take a deep breath; realize you do have options; and gather information before taking action."

. . . .

Paul's Choice

Given his nature, his upbringing, his work, his values, and his love, Paul did not even consider any other choice. He was bound to Mary, and had made an inviolable commitment to take care of her "'til death do us part."

One evening, Paul did not answer the phone when his daughter called. She telephoned several times over the next two days only to hear a busy signal. Alarmed, she finally went to the house and found both of her parents lying on the floor outside the upstairs bathroom. Paul's face was drawn into a grimace, and his skin appeared bleached and cold to the touch. A ring of white capsules surrounded his torso.

Paul had died of a sudden heart attack. Mary had poured a bottle of aspirin over Paul and then curled herself around his body, protecting him as best as she could. She was still alive.

The Aftermath

After much soul-searching, their adult children placed Mary in a nursing home and continued to visit her regularly. They were relieved that she was receiving the attention she needed and that they could restore some balance to their own lives. But they were left with the terrible questions that anyone faces in a similar situation.

Did Paul make the right choice? Did his insistence on continuing to play his role as "Big Daddy" lead to his death? Did his unwavering caretaking of Mary blind him to signs of his own body's slow shutdown? Did the sheer physical strain of caring for Mary's aging and needy body damage his heart? Should he have placed Mary in a nursing home earlier in order to preserve his own life and the remnants of their relationship? Or did he in fact choose the path that was best for both Mary and him?

We each have to wrestle with questions like these in ways that make sense for our lives and relationships. If the ill partner is unable to participate, the well partner still needs to address these questions, either alone or with a trusted advisor or family member. Even though the answers may remain elusive, asking the questions and working to find insights may ultimately provide some resolution.

Alzheimer's, like a terrorist, ignites terrible fury and sadness without providing a clear target. Can you really blame the sixteen-year-old suicide bomber? Yes, but that is not enough. You know there is a universe of complicated politics that somehow coalesced to find expression in an evil and desperate act. The partner of an Alzheimer's patient is similarly left without a clear focus for his anger and hurt. Do you indict the disease or the medical system that doesn't have a cure yet? Do you rail against the social system that doesn't yet offer a comprehensive and affordable way to maintain patients at home? Do you blame yourself or your family for not doing enough? Do you blame your partner for getting sick? You want accountability, but you also know it is not possible and that, even if it were, it would not provide full closure. You live with that, and, we hope, with forgiveness for others, compassion for yourself, and eventually acceptance that death and illness are part of life.

Postscript

No couple is prepared for the magnitude of change created by serious illness. Familiar roles are upended as illness inserts itself into daily routines and relationship patterns. Expectations must be reset as illness determines how functional the ill partner can be in terms of daily responsibilities and emotional presence. The well partner may be called upon to carry out practical chores and acts of selflessness that he never imagined would wind up in his repertoire. Typically what was once a relationship of equals becomes one of caregiver and patient. For some couples, like Emily and Wayne, illness propels them to reach greater levels of engagement. For others, like Paul and Mary, illness further deepens the patterns and values on which their relationship rested for decades.

The upheaval of having to adapt to new and potentially undesirable roles makes it easy for resentment and retreat to slip into the couple relationship. The partners are called on to make many choices every day in unaccustomed ways—choices about what needs to be done, who does what, what role each person will play, what each partner needs to do for the other. These choices can be made sympathetically, robotically, or grudgingly, from the stance of victim or bully or saint. As Dr. Wogrin said, "You can't change the illness, but you can fix the issues." Here are some suggestions for how couples can mitigate the role turbulence that illness can trigger. Where possible, couples should work together. When cognitive problems make this difficult, family members can be consulted.

- Practice "unconditional presence"—being fully present, with mind and heart, with your partner, without trying to fix anything. This creates a simple space in which both partners can, once again, be with each other as equals, as two adults joined together in sharing the sadness of illness, the old memories it awakens, and the new possibilities it generates. As Dr. Caplin said, "This [unconditional presence] is the most important thing partners can do."

- Prepare a "holding environment," an uninterrupted time in a private space in which partners (if both are able) reach out to each other with benevolence to discuss difficult questions honestly—questions such as, "How do we need to reconfigure our lives and who will do what?" Begin by agreeing that this discussion is above all a vehicle to promote well-being and to carry you to the next level of connection, and it is therefore essential that the fears and sorrows emerge, along with the practical solutions.

- Don't focus on a dreaded and uncertain future. When circumstances are unpredictable, be as concrete as possible about the few next steps.

Here are a set of activities partners (if illness permits) can engage in to clarify their new roles:

1. Set aside a time outside the turbulence to rationally discuss what strengths each person can bring to deal with daily life and medical demands. Illness forces so many unwanted burdens on us, we tend to feel overwhelmed, and that feeling can constrict our sense of our own capabilities.

2. Together, both people can write out a list of which basic activities and chores need to be done—for the household, the children, work, the illness, and each other.

3. The ill partner goes first and states what she feels able to do (knowing that this can change and may increase or decrease daily). Can she shop for groceries? No. Can she arrange for groceries to be delivered? Can she drive the kids to soccer? No. Can she call someone to arrange for transportation? The idea is to find some way for the ill person to stay engaged in the world and hold onto adult responsibilities, while accommodating to the real constraints imposed by illness. This may seem burdensome. But the more the ill person gives away, the more she fades away, and the more power the illness gains.

4. The well partner does not have to pick up whatever remains on the list. The well partner also needs to assess what his priorities and capabilities are. He may need to work overtime and may not have the time or energy for cleaning the house or helping the kids with homework. And the well partner's capabilities can also change on a daily basis.

5. After the well partner decides what responsibilities he can undertake, there will be leftovers. Then both partners think together—constructively, not blamefully—about how they can get help from an outside source to pick up these remainders. Can they hire a cleaning service twice a month? Will their insurance pay for a home health aide to bathe the ill partner? Can friends, neighbors, and family be enlisted to prepare meals, chauffeur kids, or drive the ill partner to medical appointments?

6. The most important part of doing this role inventory is not the thoroughness of the list (which can always be amended), but rather the spirit of mutual caring the couple brings to the conversation. If this activity

is done with acrimony, then the efforts each partner makes will carry the extra load of bitterness. If the preamble to this activity is, "We are both having a difficult time. Maybe we're trying too hard. Let's figure out together how we can be easy on ourselves and make it easier for each other—because we care about each other," the efforts made will be lightened by compassion.

The more the partners can infuse compassion into their new roles and into the ways they interact and make choices, the stronger they will be as individuals and as a couple, and the more resources they will have to cope with their illness situation. Tulku Thondup, visiting scholar at Harvard University and expert in Tibetan Buddhism, emphasizes the importance of compassion, without conditions, as a path to wholeness. "Compassion is a loving, caring attitude toward another without thinking 'I, me, my.'" Making role choices that are rooted in a spirit of compassion can enable both partners to mitigate the breakage that illness introduces into habitual patterns and to recreate relationship wholeness.

Part II
The Second Dimension

Balancing Act

Chapter 3

Communication:

Speaking the Unspeakable

B efore illness interrupts the couple relationship, activity can often function as a substitute for communication. Two busy people taking care of the demands of work and family slide through their days in rapid motion. They may speak in bursts of instruction, questions, and deals. "Can you pick up the kids after soccer?" "Please bring home pizza for dinner. Remember Bill's allergic to onions." "What do you want to do about the Smiths' invitation to their anniversary party?" "If you get the dry cleaning, I'll pick up the dog food."

The rare slack time is usually dedicated to conversations about pressing issues: the children's behavior, upcoming visits to the grandparents, work successes and stresses. Discussions about finances, vacations, housecleaning, and family time are the closest approximations to relationship conversations. Arguments erupt and dissipate, but they leave behind small cracks and dents that make the structure of the relationship more vulnerable to the next tempest. Genuine busyness can provide enough momentum to keep the couple operating fairly stably for years as they maintain a functional balance between efficiency and avoidance.

When circumstances or emotional crises do require a relationship readjustment and discussion, the tenor of the conversation can range from benign to skirmish to sniping to aggressive. Partners may compete with one another using volume, emotion, logic, whatever munitions they are packing, to overwhelm the other's position and be declared the winner by some illusory tribunal. A combination of silence, distance, or appeasement may serve to maintain the connection until busyness takes over again. Unless the couple has had excellent role models or therapy, they may not know how to listen with empathy and resolve conflict, skills that are rarely taught at home or at school.

Serious illness acts as a giant stop sign, halting the flow of activity that substituted for meaningful dialogue. When your usual pathways between home, work, and school are diverted to hospitals and doctors' offices, the old routines become obsolete and can no longer provide fodder for communication. When exhaustion, confusion, and anxiety fill the space that enterprise and exertion once occupied, you are forced not only to stop, but to turn inward. Suddenly, amidst the disorientation and complexity that illness brings, you look across this new terrain and find that your partner's eyes are one of the few remaining familiar anchor points. But this does not guarantee communication.

Illness, especially at the outset, tends to heighten emotion and short-circuit communication. There is so much new information bombarding you that you might become highly reactive and respond to each new byte of data with a sense of urgency, rather than taking time to ground yourselves in your connection to each other and respond thoughtfully as a team. Often the new information raises concerns about the condition and its prognosis, pushing dangerous words like diagnosis, surgery, disability, damage, malignancy, drugs, and mortality to the forefront.

Couples who are unaccustomed to maintaining dialogue about emotional matters tend to adopt one of four approaches when facing serious illness or trauma:

1. They focus entirely on the practicalities and ignore the emotional repercussions.

2. They surrender to medical authorities and follow their recommendations without much questioning.

3. They attempt to use their pre-illness, externally focused, short-burst patterns of communication, which are too shallow to address the convolutions of their current health crisis.

4. They drop into denial and avoid the situation to the extent that they can.

A further complication that can arise is that one partner may choose one approach while the other partner elects another, and thus they grow farther out of sync with each other.

However, illness can also serve as a catalyst for engaging in deeper, more authentic and more intimate forms of communication. When old methods no longer work and the situation calls for difficult decisions and adjustments, couples can learn to break the silence, put down their verbal weapons, and open up to new modes of honest dialogue. They can learn that revealing secret hopes and fears does not make you more vulnerable, but rather builds a strong bridge to your most powerful ally, your partner. They can learn that "speaking the unspeakable" makes both of you stronger.

In this chapter we meet three couples. Frances and Ted had spent years in couples' therapy learning to use new communication methods under difficult conditions. Frances's experience with fibromyalgia and her subsequent thoughts about suicide put their skills to the test. Claire and Bruce had settled into an acceptable communication rhythm that was disrupted when her ovarian cancer diagnosis alerted her to deficiencies in their relationship. Katherine and Jerry had passion, but little connection and few tools for communicating honestly outside the bedroom. When Katherine suffered a head injury in a car accident, she realized she had actually been alone for a long time.

Frances and Ted: Speaking the Unspeakable

Frances and Ted told us their story together as we sat with them around their dining room table. When Frances turned thirty-three, she started to become someone she did not know. She had always been able to count on her body to serve her will. If she wanted to ski, swim, work, make love, or sleep, her body complied. Her husband, Ted, whom she met on a ski lift, was equally reliant on his body. Doing pleasurably strenuous activities together was a fundamental part of their relationship.

At the age of thirty-three, Frances began to get signals from her body that all was not well. She felt tired as soon as she woke up in the morning, even though she had had eight hours of sleep. Most disturbing to her was that her body hurt. She felt aches and pains similar to those she experienced after a ten-mile hike. At times, when Ted caressed her thick, dark hair or massaged her shoulders, she yelped in pain.

Frances tried to ignore her symptoms, but over the next six months they got worse. She was tired all the time, which made it difficult for her to concentrate at work as a lawyer and caused her to become abrupt with Ted or avoid him altogether. Ted showed his concern by inviting her to participate in the activities they enjoyed, which had often worked in the past when Frances was in a bad mood. Now, however, Frances was too tired or too much in pain to engage, and too confused and worried to explain. Their world had changed, and they didn't know why.

Learning to Communicate

Ted came from a family whose motto had been, "Don't rock the boat." Frances's family believed in throwing emotional spitballs at each other without taking responsibility for the damage. After a few months of marriage, years before her symptoms started, their boat was rocking, and they knew they needed help to learn how to steady it through communication, rather than depending on their familial legacies of evasion and silence. They entered couples' therapy.

Through couples' therapy they learned the crucial lesson that what doesn't get addressed doesn't go away; it goes underground and continues to create ripples. Their new motto became, "Always speak the unspeakable. What doesn't get spoken gets acted out." This meant that when Ted read the sports section of the local newspaper at the dinner table, Frances, instead of huffing and clanging silverware, would say, "Ted, I know you like to read about sports, but I cooked a nice dinner for us, and I feel unappreciated when you read the paper while we're eating. I'd much rather we talk or even be quiet, but at least let's be together without distractions. Would you mind reading the paper later?" It took months for Frances to learn to express her wants in this way—owning her feelings, showing empathy for Ted, not blaming or belittling him, and asking clearly for what she wanted.

It took Ted a little longer to recognize that strong feelings underlay some of his behaviors. When he absentmindedly walked out in the middle of a conversation or forgot to pick up the food order Frances had called in to the market or told her at 6:00 p.m. on a Friday night that he was playing poker with the boys, he could never understand Frances's ensuing upset. He would wait numbly until her rant subsided, then say, "Sorry, I just forgot," or "I didn't think it mattered," and then he would just stop talking.

The couples therapist helped Ted realize that his "sorry" was a deflecting maneuver rather than a real apology and that underneath his forgetfulness was a stew of anger, resentment, and fear. Frances's emotions, especially her anger and disappointment, were so foreign to him that they frightened him. He withdrew at the first signs of an argument. Ted learned to say to Frances, "I have a hard time really listening to you when you raise your voice in anger. You have every right to be angry, but it does frighten me and make me want to retreat. Do you think you could try to tell me what's upsetting you in a quieter voice? I really do want to understand."

Four Principles for Excellent Communication

David Bohm, quantum physicist and philosopher, wrote a seminal essay, "On Dialogue," in which he posited that through open dialogue, new meanings and new possibilities can emerge, which then become shared and serve to hold people together. While Bohm's approach was originally meant for groups, it is also relevant for creating a context for empathic communication between partners. Here are four principles for dialoguing rooted in Bohm's philosophy:

· · · · · · · · · · ·

EMPATHIC COMMUNICATION

1. **No decisions will be made in the conversation.** There needs to be an empty space in which the participants are not obligated to make assessments and come to conclusions. It is only in an empty, agenda-free space that participants can be free to speak openly.

2. **Each person agrees to suspend judgment** so that ideas can be exchanged and heard without being assessed as good or bad. Judgment brings out defensiveness and argument and shuts down clear listening.

3. Participants are as honest and transparent as possible. Each person speaks his or her truth, even though it might feel awkward or even frightening to do so. The second principle, no judgment, helps foster the environment that makes this level of honesty possible.

4. Participants in the conversation try to build on each other's ideas. To build on another's idea, you must first listen and absorb it sufficiently. To listen, you must step away from your position, suspend any hostility and rigidity, and enter into the other's perspective.[1]

This is empathy.

. . . .

The Hardest Conversation

During the year that Frances and Ted were in therapy, they learned to recognize their own emotions and to appreciate the subtle and volatile ways their feelings could inter-twine and ignite each other. They learned how to communicate with honesty about their needs and with empathy for each other's feelings. Over time, they could even say to each other, "I don't want to be with you today," or "Someone at work is flirting with me and I'm enjoying it," or "I'm feeling lonely—can you come over here and hold me?" without fearing that a bottomless pit would open up beneath their feet. They learned to speak the unspeakable.

Frances, however, continued to deteriorate. Her pain and exhaustion were debili-tating. She spent a year making the rounds of doctors and specialists. Too often, she left their offices feeling misunderstood and subtly blamed for her state. Some suggested she increase her vitamin intake. Others implied that her complaints were psychological. She took a leave of absence from work and stopped going out with friends. Most nights, Ted held her as she cried in frustration and pain. An optimist by nature, he tried repeat-edly to persuade her that the next specialist might have the answer.

Trapped in agony, Frances began to contemplate suicide secretly. The past was

---

[1] Wikipedia, http://en.wikipedia.org/wiki/Bohm_Dialogue

over; the present was unbearable; and the future held no promise of relief. Ironically, in her desperate state, the contemplation of suicide became her only ray of hope, but it was not a hope she believed she could share.

Frances hated keeping this secret from Ted, but she feared that this was one "unspeakable" he would not be able to tolerate. She was consumed with her internal debate—to tell or not to tell—and this was draining whatever strength she had left. There was no room left for connecting with Ted on any level. The more she remained in this state, the lonelier she felt and the more suicide seemed like the solution.

After struggling with this alone for several weeks, Frances realized that, as hard as it would be for Ted to hear, she had to share her fantasies about a "suicidal cure" with him. She asked him to take the morning off from work at his architecture firm since that was the time of day when her stamina was at its highest. They sat side by side on their living room couch. Not knowing how else to tell him, Frances simply said, "I have been thinking about suicide." The moment the words came out of her mouth, her body relaxed.

After years of practice at empathic communication, Ted did not react by discounting or diminishing or challenging her feelings. He did not say, "No! You can't do that. You don't know what you're saying." He looked into her eyes and calmly said, "You've clearly been hurting for a long time, physically and emotionally. I can understand that you would think about suicide. Any normal person in your situation would. Tell me about it." He listened for the next hour while Frances revealed the extent of her misery at having lost the life she loved with him, her rage at her body, which had become her enemy, and her despair over ever regaining a life worth living.

When she stopped, they held one another and cried together. The misery became a shared pain joining them and no longer a secret burden keeping them apart. Feeling her world uplifted by Ted's strength and compassion, Frances no longer needed to hold on so tightly to suicide as her only liberator. They both knew suicide was an option, but they could place it outside the space they had just created: available if needed, but not overpowering their spirit.

Dr. Carol Wogrin, Director of the National Center for Death Education, affirms, "Choosing to end life is not all that common. But it is common to think about it and know you have the option and will have help should that be the choice. To actually go through with it is rarer, especially when the person's emotional and practical needs are being met."

Soon after this conversation, Frances was evaluated by a rheumatologist who had several patients with similar complaints. He asked her a series of diagnostic questions that mapped almost exactly to her symptoms. He gave her condition a name—fibromyalgia—and explained how they would treat it together. Frances felt hope for the first time in over a year.

Over the course of the next three years, Frances learned to manage this chronic condition through a combination of medications, meditation, and alternative methods. She and Ted don't have the life they once knew, but they are both quick to say that their life now, while different, is wonderful.

Claire and Bruce: Reweaving the Fabric

Claire invited us to meet her in her local coffee shop to tell us the story of her illness experience. At the time she was living with her partner, Bruce.

Claire and Bruce had each left unhappy, long-term marriages five years before they met. Their divorces were messy and antagonistic and left them battered, wary of emotional entanglement. Since then they had dated little and preferred to spend time with their adult children. They were introduced through a mutual friend who had grown tired of listening to their complaints about loneliness and the failings of the opposite sex. The friend thought they would be a good match and arranged for them to exchange phone numbers.

After several weeks of nervous avoidance and phone tag, they spoke and decided to meet for coffee at a local cafe. They immediately connected over the similarities of their unhappy marriage and ugly divorce experiences. The more they detailed their grievances, the more they grew to believe that they had found someone who truly understood and would never replicate the injustices they had suffered. Each felt an upsurge of hope at having found a potential partner completely unlike the previous one—someone who, having suffered the wounds, would not inflict them.

The Communication Pattern Gets Set

They dated for a year and found their initial impressions to be true. Neither one was the least like the other's previous marriage partner, and this was so reassuring that it sufficed to become the foundation for a committed relationship. However, "difference from the prior partner" as the seedbed for a new relationship is not a secure platform on which to build. Claire and Bruce ignored the warning signs of other emotional differences and imbalances that would, over the next few years, introduce fissures into their relationship.

Claire had always been quick to make decisions and act on them. She decided on her major during her freshman year at college and never wavered from that choice. She shopped for groceries with equal determination and a prepared list, and usually completed this task in twenty minutes, even on a crowded Sunday afternoon. In her relationship with Bruce she quickly became the leader, and he complied.

Claire decided when they would move in together. She found their first home and chose the furniture. Bruce had no strong opinions on these matters and was happy to leave these choices to Claire, who also established the routines in their home. She shopped and cooked and gardened. He ran unanticipated errands. They both cleaned. Decisions that arose—about finances, investments, invitations, family gatherings—were Claire's to make and Bruce's to accept. Amiable and adaptable, Bruce was comfortable with Claire taking the lead. Bruce was content focusing on his work as a computer specialist and his love of performing music with his jazz band.

Claire felt no need for marriage. She thought that living together would suit them just fine, and Bruce agreed. At times, Claire felt traces of resentment about the load she carried. At times, Bruce showed a flicker of indignation that his opinions never mattered. They both ignored these signals and carried on.

Their communication was largely instructional and initiated by Claire. When organizing wasn't required and they had unstructured time together, they chatted about movies, books, politics, the weather, and other topics. They could enjoy each other's company and, when power and acquiescence weren't involved, they could talk cheerfully and companionably. However, they had no language to name and discuss the ways in which they were beginning to collide, so they avoided all reference to their differences.

Illness Changes the Game

Four years into their relationship, at the age of forty-two, Claire was diagnosed with uterine cancer and needed a hysterectomy. She continued to stay in control of her medical experience and her relationship right up until the day after her surgery. Then she hit the wall. The abdominal surgery, coupled with seismic shifts in her hormones, left her incapacitated physically and emotionally. She felt as if she couldn't control a pencil, much less her life or anyone else's. For the first time she wanted someone else to take charge of the world and take care of her. She began looking to Bruce to fill this void.

Bruce appeared to Claire to be bewildered by her neediness and at a loss about how to change his behavior. He asked his adult daughter to stay with them to help take care of Claire. Claire unfortunately found his daughter to be unhelpful and defiant. When Claire asked her to get a cup of tea or to change the bed linen, the daughter stared at her and walked away. Bruce buckled under his daughter's every demand and spent more time placating her than either of them spent helping Claire.

Claire experienced a degree of anger she had never known before. She had meticulously sculpted her world so that she could control its elements. Her illness and her surgery stole this illusory power and left her submerged in helplessness—the helplessness she had managed to avoid all her life.

Ghosts from the Past

As the oldest child in her family Claire took on the role of "parent" to her siblings. This is not an unusual situation and can result from a number of circumstances. Claire's father was a brilliant physicist, and her mother was a relentless volunteer in her community. Their attention was focused outside the nuclear family, and they trusted Claire to manage the home front.

When adults are absent or dysfunctional, which may occur because of illness, addiction, or major life distractions (as was the case with Claire's parents), the oldest child is often bequeathed the mantle of responsibility to maintain at least a semblance of domestic stability. This child may take charge of running the house and looking after other children. She prepares meals from whatever sparse supplies are available in the kitchen, makes sure the younger children bathe and get to school, and may even clean up the mess left by a drug-addicted parent or intervene in alcohol-infused battles between parents. This child is granted too much power and responsibility at too early an age. As an adult, she overfunctions and spends her energy trying to keep the universe in its proper orbit, at the expense of being able to trust and depend on others. Becoming vulnerable is experienced as a precursor to obliteration.

From early childhood, Claire had taken on a "parenting assistant" role in her family of origin. As the oldest of four siblings, she often took charge. She could never afford to capitulate to helplessness or acknowledge her own neediness. She often felt that hers was the strength that bound her family together.

Her illness and resulting infirmity became a breach through which decades of pent-up yearning to be cared for and kept safe burst through as a roar of anger. Claire did not understand the psychology of her unleashed neediness. All she knew was that she was hurting, and that it was her turn to be taken care of.

Unfortunately, Bruce had either been trained or had learned with Claire to stand back and let the powerful women take charge. Neither one understood the mechanisms for engaging in self-understanding or had the communication tools for jointly analyzing and adapting to their new situation. They were babes in the dark relationship woods.

In order to survive, Claire lashed out. Since Bruce wasn't nurturing her, she said to him, "Get out!" Those were the only words she could put to the rage and sorrow of her emotional losses, old ones and new ones all rolled into one.

One neurologist described a similar couple whose relationship equilibrium shattered after the male partner underwent surgery. This doctor said, "For couples, illness can be the stress test that you flunk."

Changing the Pattern

Bruce and Claire separated for six months, after which Bruce asked to come back. They both decided that couples' therapy would be a prerequisite for reconciliation. This was the first joint decision they had ever made, and it became the precursor for learning how to have an "intentional" dialogue, in which both partners listen to each other with empathy, as equals, not as combatants.

They worked very hard in therapy. Claire had to learn to recognize and express her needs rather than attempt to control situations to prevent herself from feeling needy. Once she could ask Bruce for help or attention, he was eager to offer it and grew skilled at responding. He had a harder time initiating caring and an even harder time understanding his own emotional rhythms. Bruce never seemed to reach a level of deep personal awareness, but he excelled at responding to Claire's newly open expression of her needs. Claire felt better being nurtured, and was able to release some control, and Bruce was happy that they were back together. They succeeded in reaching a more sustainable equilibrium.

Katherine and Jerry: Lust at First Sight

Katherine began her story by saying that when she met Jerry, it was lust at first sight. They were both twenty-one when they met on a beach in Puerto Rico. He was the first man she had dated who took her out to dinner. She was the first woman he had dated who understood what a two-point conversion play is in a football game.

From the beginning, their relationship was troubled. Katherine was too innocent and accommodating, and Jerry turned out to be a liar and a philanderer. The night she moved in with him, he invited two of his ex-girlfriends to visit. She waited in the bedroom with excited anticipation and growing annoyance while he "entertained" the women downstairs. That night they had the first of many fights.

Fighting and sex became the couple's primary forms of communication. The pattern would begin with Katherine seeking attention from Jerry. Jerry would either ignore her gestures or explode and berate her for being too demanding. Katherine would escalate and argue louder. Jerry would turn into a sheet of hard, cold glass. Nothing Katherine threw could stick to it, and no emotion Jerry might be feeling would materialize. Only in the bedroom were they on the same wavelength.

At other times, especially when they went out in public, Jerry could be affectionate and attentive. He would take her arm, adjust her coat collar to protect her from the wind, and kiss her playfully on the cheek. Even at home there were moments when he would massage her feet or bring her a cup of tea. Then suddenly, as if a switch had been flicked, he would berate her verbally, call her horrible names, and belittle her in the areas where she felt most insecure.

Eventually they married. As the marriage progressed and she and Jerry had two children, Katherine tried to be the pacifier and to "make things right." She was also financially dependent on Jerry, who had insisted she stay at home and leave the providing to him. She felt trapped and humiliated and began to suspect that Jerry was having affairs. Katherine continually internalized his emotional abuse and experienced it as a deadly confirmation of the defects she tried to hide, the ones her own father had instilled in her and conditioned her to accept.

The Past Lives in the Present

Katherine's mother died when she was seven years old. Throughout her childhood, her father threatened to abandon her. When he got upset with her for leaving her toys in the living room, for not cleaning the countertop after she prepared her own breakfast or for having new shoes that squeaked, he would say, "I never wanted you, your mother did. Here's a list of people who will take you in when I leave." The seeds for seeing herself as bad and unwanted were planted early and deeply. For Katherine, conflict became equated with abandonment and terror. For three decades she did everything she could to appease the people in her life and to suppress arguments that she believed would lead to desertion. She had been trained to be the perfect mate for a manipulative partner.

The Accident

A few weeks before Katherine's and Jerry's fifteenth anniversary, Katherine was driving on a major highway en route to visit her aunt. Suddenly she noticed that the cars ahead of her had slowed almost to a stop. She immediately stomped on her brakes and saw in her rearview mirror that the car behind her was not slowing down. She heard the shriek of metal crashing against metal as the other car plunged into her car. Her neck snapped back as her car spun around. Her first thought was that Jerry would be angry about having to drive two hours to get her. Her second thought was, "God, don't let me die."

Jerry met her at the hospital where the ambulance took her. He was actually concerned and nurturing. She was sent home with a cervical collar and some aspirin. Jerry remained solicitous for the first six weeks, until he realized that Katherine's condition was not a short-term matter and that her pain, fatigue, and confusion might last.

Ten months after the accident, Katherine was diagnosed with a frontal lobe brain injury, which would continue to affect her ability to process information, find the correct words to express a thought, and filter out distractions. She also suffered pain in her upper back and neck. By this time, Jerry had decided that since Katherine looked normal, nothing was really wrong with her, and he assumed she was using her complaints as a maneuver to get his attention. He dropped the sympathy and returned to belligerence and adultery.

Invisible Illness

Like millions of others, Katherine belongs to a class of people who suffer from an "invisible illness." Invisible illness refers to real medical conditions that can deeply affect an individual's health and daily functioning, but which have no outward indicators. If someone walks with a cane or has a service dog or is wearing a head scarf to cover hair loss, we know they have a health condition, and we treat them with support and understanding. We can see the evidence of illness, and our compassion activates. We ask, "How are you doing?" or "Can I help?"

When people have an invisible illness, like a brain injury, chronic pain, or some autoimmune condition, their outward appearances don't necessarily change even though their suffering may be great. Others may respond to the person's normal, even healthy, appearance and think that the ill person is exaggerating, malingering, or trying to get attention. The refrain people with invisible illnesses too often hear is, "But you look fine." The hidden implication is: If you were really ill, you would bear the visible marks like stigmata on your face or body. Without the marks, the person with invisible illness loses credibility. Not only does the ill person have to cope with the demands of illness, she also has to convince family, friends, coworkers, and employers of her genuine physical and mental limitations.

Illness Makes the Cracks More Evident

Psychologist and grief specialist Dr. Ester Shapiro said, "How a couple has been tested prior to the illness, how they came through before, brings either strength or fear to the illness experience." A holistic psychotherapist we spoke to described a situation like Katherine's and Jerry's, in which the woman had always been the productive, organized one, on top of it all. When she struggled with illness and needed help, her partner continued to be as unavailable as he was before. "The spouses who weren't there before, with illness, can become even more absent," said this therapist. Katherine's and Jerry's history of coping with both major and minor issues was brutal and punishing. They were not well situated to deal lovingly with her brain trauma.

Jerry's main response to Katherine's brain damage was irritation. He often said to her in a sarcastic tone, "You sure seem smart to me. If you have a brain injury then I must have one too." He saw no evidence of damage, and therefore could not accept the symptoms as anything other than pretense. When Katherine discovered that he had been having an affair with a friend of hers, one that started while she was still hospitalized, a volcano erupted within her. She spewed out words she didn't think she would ever have the courage to say: "I can't live with you anymore. You need to sort out what's going on with you and find someplace else to live while you do it." She hired a lawyer and began divorce proceedings.

Katherine then suffered a fear she had never known before. The fear that preceded an onslaught of Jerry's abuse was benign compared to the terror of being alone. It took her many months and help from a psychotherapist specializing in brain injury to remember that she was no longer a seven-year-old motherless child, dependent on an abusive father for all her needs. What she did find was a strong, assertive, and courageous sense of herself hidden underneath the many layers of protection she had constructed. As she learned to rely on her own strength and to moderate her environment to accommodate her brain injury, she started to feel centered and happy.

Katherine continues to struggle to create love and safety in the relationships she has had since the divorce. She carries the lessons from her failed marriage with her: "If the relationship is not good in the best circumstances, it won't be good in the worst. Couples should examine the loose stones in their foundation and strengthen them now, because you never know what and when something will happen. They don't call it 'an accident' for no reason."

Postscript

Illness compels us to communicate. From the first moment of diagnosis, the couple must talk about subjects that are far outside their customary purview. And they must do so under conditions of strong emotion and pervasive uncertainty. Even couples who have developed good communication stumble. Couples who have had communication breakdowns pre-illness will find that illness strains their habits and forces them to cultivate new ones or to grow apart. The time to proactively build strong communication channels is now, because you can never predict when illness or accident will arrive. Rev. John Buehrens, Unitarian Universalist minister, puts it this way: "There is randomness though all existence. A virus can mutate. Evolution has a bias towards diversity. Illness or an accident comes out of this randomness. All one can do is to stand ready to receive." Having a solid communication platform and practice at holding difficult conversations helps you to "stand ready." There are several approaches couples can use to communicate authentically:

- Understand that what doesn't get addressed through open communication does not go away. It goes underground and continues to create ripples. Not talking about your fear or loneliness does not make you less afraid or less lonely. In fact, not talking, putting a lid on emotions through silence, usually serves to increase their potency. Hidden emotions tend to leak out in symbolic ways: getting overly upset over a broken dish, worrying that the (healthy) cat has a serious infection, getting angry at your partner for coming home fifteen minutes late. As long as there is no history of partner abuse, sharing your deep feelings with each other creates healing connections.

- To have open, honest communication about difficult topics, it helps to have some ground rules: 1) Declare a time and place for talk without the need to solve problems and make decisions. 2) Discuss without judging or criticizing. 3) Each partner "speaks the unspeakable," as Ted and Frances learned to do. Say your truth aloud even if it is uncomfortable to do so. 4) Listen and respond with empathy by entering into your partner's experience.

Ideally, you focus on deepening the candor and intimacy of your communication before illness arrives. As Katherine wisely advises: "If the relationship is not good in the best circumstances, it won't be good in the worst. Couples should examine the loose stones in their foundation and strengthen them now because you never know what and when something will happen." If something has already happened, it is never too late to learn how to express your innermost hopes and fears, joys and vexations to your partner (and to listen empathically to his) with honesty and compassion.

Chapter 4

Together and Apart: Creating Balance

I llness or injury strips away the illusion that many couples have of complete union with the loved one. The cruel realities of pain, disability, or deterioration focus a laser light on our essential aloneness. When we have a serious illness, we understand that we are the only ones in our bodies, and no matter how much others may love us, they can never fully enter our experiences. Despite this, we may still be able to find connection with our loved one, even as we stand alone.

However, the structure of connection is as different as one couple is from another. For some couples the commitment to stay together means marriage (or some form of commitment ceremony) followed by living together. For others, commitment can take other forms. For many couples, that structure can change as the illness evolves. The intense demands of illness can force some couples to seek physical separation in order to find the respite they need to recharge and sustain the relationship. Other couples immerse themselves so deeply in the illness that disease becomes the basis for their connection. They no longer have any intimate bonds outside of the domain of illness. They stay together, but they become cloistered from the rest of the world. For still other couples, the burden of illness combined with an already damaged relationship is too much to carry, and their connection is severed.

In this chapter, we meet two couples whose relationships ebbed and flowed with the currents of long-term illness and deterioration. Each couple is of a different generation and marital status, and each charted the course of their relationship in very different ways. During their journeys, both couples found hope and healing, even through the ultimate separation of death. In coping with illness, each couple found the unique closeness-distance pattern that reflected their individual needs and their levels of tolerance as a couple.

Marian and Arthur: Learning to Adapt

Marian was a young woman sheltered by her family and community, and she was looking for excitement. When, in her twenties, she met her first husband, she was intoxicated by his physical elegance and urbane wit. She knew she would marry him the evening he put his arms around her waist and whirled her around the dance floor. Wrapped in his embrace, she felt protected and exhilarated, sensations she had rarely experienced in tandem. Dazzled, she married with her "happy ever after" assumptions intact. Her first husband, however, deceived her. He never told her that he suffered from an incurable, life-threatening disease. Even after he became bedridden, he never disclosed the full nature of his illness. Only after his death did she learn from his family and his doctor what he had been concealing. He died at the age of thirty-six of the complications of Huntington's disease (a genetic disorder), leaving her a young widow with two daughters aged three and five, and her innocent trust in men and relationships shattered. After his death, she was determined to find greater stability and honesty the next time.

Writing a New Story

We spoke to Marian by telephone. She now lives in an assisted care facility in Quebec, the Canadian province where she grew up. She apologized for being unavailable at the outset of our appointed time and explained that a neighbor needed her advice. She joked about putting her old social worker skills to good use amongst her current community of friends. It was clear, even from that first moment, that Marian was actively living her life.

In a firm, enthusiastic voice, she launched into her story. She had met Arthur, her second husband, at the age of thirty-two, after having been widowed for a year.

They began dating regularly, and Arthur quickly decided that marriage was in their future. Between dinners they spent hours on the phone, and Marian remembers thinking, "Well, here's a man you can talk to, and someone you can trust." Best of all, he was healthy. Given her experience with her first husband, these were especially significant impressions for Marian to form. However, the health requirement was an impossible one to fulfill, as Marian found out.

· · · · · · · · · · ·

DR. ABBY CAPLIN — BRINGING AWARENESS TO OLD PATTERNS

Abby Caplin, M.D., M.A., a psychotherapist who works with people dealing with illness, is alert to the "legacies" people bring with them into the illness experience. "Previous patterns come alive with illness," she says. She offers the example of a couple in her care: "Whenever she got angry, he felt like a small boy with his angry mother. In response to that anger he withdrew. His withdrawal reminded her of her distant father, and she began to feel like a rejected little girl." The key, Dr. Caplin emphasizes, is to "bring awareness to the pattern." Without awareness, the old cycles keep repeating, and the couple stays stuck in outdated roles and unproductive routines. Becoming aware of these patterns enables the couple to make more adult choices about their reactions.

· · · · · · · · · · ·

Marian believed she had found the steadfast protector and companion she sought, just as Arthur had found someone to love and look after his daughter. They married and set up household with Marian's two daughters and Arthur's one. Trying to blend two families with five differing sets of personalities and exigencies while establishing a spousal relationship was "the hardest job" Marian ever did.

After their daughters were fully grown, Marian and Arthur grew closer and reignited their premarital energy. They retired, and with a wild freedom they had both missed due to early marriage and childrearing, they decided to carry out their equivalent of piercing body parts and hopping on a Harley. They divested themselves of extraneous material goods, bought a motor home, and hit Route 66.

For twenty-five years they traveled back and forth across the United States, never heading in a straight line for more than a state or two. Periodically, they docked in Florida and remained there for several months at a time. While they were always together, they also developed separate interests. Arthur often read quietly or did T'ai Chi and encouraged Marian to pursue whatever intrigued her. Arranging flowers, socializing with their campground neighbors, studying maps, building computer skills, and keeping up with news of her children and grandchildren became Marian's avocations. Marian described these transcontinental years as the best part of their marriage. "We had to have a good marriage to live together well in such a tiny space."

Breaking the Contract

When Marian was in her late sixties and Arthur in his late seventies, she noticed that while Arthur still maintained immaculate care of his person, he no longer liked to take responsibility for business matters or trip planning—two domains that he had administered with pride and ease. He began to get lost while driving on familiar winding roads in Florida, and could no longer track payment of bills. In addition to these early signs of mental disorganization, the diabetes he had contracted in his sixties was beginning to affect his eyesight.

As Arthur's mental and physical changes picked up momentum, he and Marian slipped into the role changes so familiar to couples who live with illness. Marian became the travel director and keeper of the maps, both geographic and social. She took care of all negotiations with the outside world, while Arthur focused on his self-care regimen and acquiesced to her decisions.

When Arthur was in his eighties, their children encouraged the couple to settle permanently in Florida to be near reliable health care providers. Marian took full responsibility for finding a home, selling the trailer, and managing their relocation. Three days after they moved into their new home, Marian had a stroke. She believed that the stroke was a result of the emotional duress of watching her reliable, trustworthy, and healthy husband deteriorate, coupled with the fatigue and strain of negotiating their resettlement. This duress was particularly charged for Marian because she, in part, felt that Arthur was breaking his contract to remain healthy.

Arthur had already been in a "vague state" before Marian's stroke, and being separated from her while she was in the hospital further corroded his life-management skills. Their children took turns coming to Florida to help out, but Arthur steadily became more disoriented and confused, until he could no longer find his way from the entrance of their housing complex to his own unit.

This was not what she had bargained for. She had already suffered unforeseen abandonment by her first husband. Her second had been chosen largely for his durability. He was to be the rock to her river—to be stable and consistent while she flowed in new, experimental directions. In the hospital, frightened of the consequences of her stroke, she looked to Arthur for emotional support he could not provide.

As a Canadian citizen, Marian had to relocate to Canada in order to receive the rehabilitation services she needed. On the day they were to leave Florida, Arthur was found by a neighbor sitting on the front steps of their home with a suitcase filled with frozen dinners. Marian was so preoccupied with yet another relocation and her own ill health that she could not register how far he had deteriorated. She was impatient with his unavailability and seeming obstructiveness. But she was not yet ready to attach the proper label and all its implications to his behavior.

It is not unusual for family members and for the patient with some form of dementia to collude, often for years, in denying the patient's mental and physical decline. Forgetful, obstinate, feisty, distracted are adjectives that substitute for speaking aloud the word "dementia." The terror of losing your mind while still in your body, the anguish of watching the person you chose to love above all others slowly fade beyond recognition are agonies no one can integrate without the protection of denial. Marian sought shelter in denial from what she feared might be true.

"After I was in the hospital and then in rehabilitation for two months, he had already begun to deteriorate, and I wasn't quite sure what was happening to him," said Marian. "We never reconnected as a team after that time, and maybe we weren't terribly connected even immediately before the stroke. I was doing all the managing. He seemed to be in some other space a lot of the time."

Marian believed that Arthur betrayed their contract by developing dementia. Marian claimed, "He was not the man I married. When I needed him he just wasn't there, and this made me sometimes disappointed, sometimes worried, and occasionally even angry. He fell forty times in two years, for example!"

· · · · · · · · · · ·

DR. CAROL WOGRIN — ONE ILLNESS, DIFFERENT EXPERIENCES

"Long-term couples have agreed-upon patterns of communication and responsibilities," says Carol Wogrin, Psy.D., R.N., a nurse and clinical psychologist who helps families live with illnesses that lead to death and significant loss, including disability. "We choose partners who complement us," says Wogrin. "One carries the emotional tasks and one carries the strategic tasks. But illness changes everything. The illness is not the same for both people and each person in the couple will be grieving in a different way. One person is experiencing the change in his body; the other is experiencing a change in the person she loves." Arthur's problem was his dementia, while Marian's problem was Arthur's abandonment of her—an abandonment that carried the extra load of betrayal of their unspoken agreement. Couples therapy, Wogrin believes, should help couples understand that each person is working on a different problem. "If they think they are solving the same problem, they will be frustrated."

· · · · · · · · · · ·

Finding Balance

As Arthur deteriorated, Marian knew that she was not the kind of wife who could sit passively by her husband's bedside while offering support, nor could she take on the repetitive, demanding tasks of providing for his daily care. In addition, since he had abrogated their contract by getting sick, she felt justified in focusing on her own life while attending to his basic needs from a distance. She arranged for Arthur to enter a nursing home. She continued to pay the bills and hired a sitter to visit him regularly and give her regular status reports. She also spent time with him, made sure he was being well taken care of, and provided him with clean, comfortable clothing and furnishings.

She focused on her own needs and her relationships with friends in her assisted living community. She helped to establish and lead two volunteer knitting groups that make blankets for homeless children in a shelter, became the chair of the residents' council, and organized group Scrabble games. She sometimes played Scrabble four times a day, saying, "It keeps the mind alive." She also used her computer to keep abreast of local and international news.

After two years in the nursing home, Arthur had steadily deteriorated and lost most of his cognitive ability as well as control over his bodily functions. "I had a responsibility to make sure he was being well taken care of, but I knew I couldn't be the person to do it myself, and he didn't demand it," said Marian. They were still able to have some kind of connection, despite is limitations. "One day, Arthur said to me, 'This marriage was a good idea. It worked out very well with the girls.' I was pleased to hear that."

After Arthur died, Marian felt almost relieved. "Watching him go downhill slowly and gently made it much easier for me," she said. "It was not a shock when he died, and I was relieved that he did not suffer. He never complained, and it was a very easy transition. He never said, 'Why me?' They adored him at the nursing home." Looking back, Marian has the following advice, both from her own experience as well as her training as a social worker: "Don't try to go it alone if you are the well partner. Get help; there is plenty of help around. In a way, my having the stroke was lucky, because it pushed me to get the help I needed to take care of Arthur."

Hard Choices

In the nursing home, Arthur was safe and well looked after. Marian found a balance between caregiver and survivor that worked well for her. Perhaps this balance enabled Marian to be as attentive to Arthur as she was.

Those who must make last-phase-of-life decisions for another are bound to rationalize some aspects of their choices. It is common to hear decision-makers use phrases that contain both truth and justification, such as: "At least he is no longer suffering," or "At least he is well cared for," or "He had no more quality of life." Living with the aftermath of these final choices would be nearly impossible if the well partner had to carry terrible guilt and remorse. And if the well partner is to maintain a caring relationship with the ill partner as he declines, the well partner has to create the physical and emotional circumstances that enable her to feel secure enough to summon the will and energy to dedicate to care. Marian was able to find that balance.

After Arthur's death, Marian continued to live an active life. Three years after he passed away, Marian said, "I think I've adjusted and accommodated myself very well. I'm in the right place, a safe place to be. I have friends. I'm dealing with my own physical problems. I am content."

Niles and Esmé: Awakened Love

This is a very different story. Whereas Marian and Arthur's path was fairly straight with a few curves, the path Niles and Esmé took through illness was a series of bewildering curlicues. But, as with all stories in this book, even the ones that we initially believe are most foreign to our experience, we may still find, as with the following story told by Niles, small mirrors in which to see hints of our lives reflected and lessons to be learned.

Niles and Esmé met at a graduate school party. Niles was immediately captivated by Esmé, an international student from Morocco, as she held court in a corner of the room, smoking and expounding brilliantly on literature and politics. They began a passionate affair, but after a few months Esmé's self-centeredness, volatile temper, and cocaine habit began to cloud Niles's initial infatuation with her, and he decided to break off the relationship.

Niles was an extremely shy person from an emotionally subdued, patrician family in which he felt overshadowed by his accomplished parents and older brothers. He had initially been attracted to Esme's exotic aura and her indifference to social norms—qualities that would have made his family squirm, and that soon began to disturb him, too. "She was too different," he said. "The screaming fights at 2:00 a.m. when I told her I wanted us to break up were exhausting. I wondered what the neighbors were thinking."

Cowed by Esmé's fury, Niles agreed to postpone the breakup for a few months, until her scheduled departure for study in Europe. During that time, she was diagnosed with lupus (an autoimmune disorder with an uncertain prognosis) and demanded that Niles stay with her. When he resisted, she threatened suicide. He felt trapped.

Bound by Old Patterns

Niles had led a relatively sheltered life, attached to a mother who, to him, embodied the perfect woman. She had impeccable manners, moved with grace, had tidy hair, and never swore. She died of cancer when Niles was in his twenties, before he had a chance to offer her a final goodbye. "The family never discussed her illness," he remembered. "She had a 'stiff upper lip' attitude and wanted to preserve normalcy and dignity until the end."

When Esmé became sick and threatened suicide if Niles left her, he was overcome with memories of his mother's illness and death and his own lost opportunity to say goodbye. From that moment on, Niles was bound to Esmé—not by love, but by an exorbitant and misshapen sense of obligation, filled with silent ghosts from the past. Each of Esmé's symptomatic episodes represented an opportunity for him to be present in a way he had not been able to do with his mother. "Esme was adept at jumping from crisis to crisis in her life, and I have a soft spot for damsels in distress," said Niles ruefully. This soft spot turned into a long-term quagmire. For twenty years Niles lived alone, supported Esmé financially, and came to her aid when she became frightened in the middle of the night. He never married or had a serious relationship, because Esmé still considered him her "boyfriend."

Psychologist Ester Shapiro said, "If you're working with old scripts, you are not being responsive to current changing circumstances." However, Dr. Shapiro affirmed, "It's never too late to have a happy ending—to revisit old ghosts and put them to rest." Unfortunately, Niles remained haunted and therefore controlled by his past for a very long time.

Esmé constantly urged Niles to marry her, and he always refused. "She had utterly alluring sides to her personality, but other sides of her had uncontrollable rage that was directed at the world and occasionally at me. I was drawn by the attractive parts of her, but did not feel that I loved her and did not want to be married to her." Still, he continued to devote much of his life to her care. "I had always thought that I would marry and have children," he said. "I do regret that it did not happen."

A Change in Course

During the last three years of her life, Esmé's condition deteriorated to the extent that she required full-time assistance in daily tasks. She refused to enter a facility, and relied on home health care during the day. Niles began to spend every night at her apartment, arriving after work, staying in the guest room, and helping her eat, bathe, use the bathroom, and get in and out of bed during the night.

Life went on in this vein for several years, until the doctors finally said that Esmé was near death. "They told me she had only a couple of days to live," said Niles. "I wanted to try to make her last days happier and knew that marriage to me was what she had wanted all these years." So he brought out a wedding ring that had been his family heirloom, arranged for a justice of the peace to come to the house, and organized a marriage ceremony. Esmé was in bed, her mother was with her, and two home health aides acted as witnesses. During the ceremony, Esmé gave what Niles describes as "a public oration." "It was touching and genuine and heartfelt, and I felt gratified that I could make her so happy," he said.

The wedding had what Niles describes as "an incredible effect" on Esmé. She rallied, began to eat and became stronger. She did not die. She changed her last name to his and spent long minutes looking at her ring. She lived for nine more months.

During this time, Niles felt his emotions toward her change. "After the wedding our relationship became very different. I would show up after work as usual, the logistics didn't change, but there was a sense that I was going to be there till the end, and her awareness of that permanence had a real effect," said Niles. "There were more kisses and gestures of love. I felt more physically and emotionally affectionate—even though there hadn't been a sexual relationship for years." During the nine months after the wedding, Niles described the awakening of a dormant love. "Until she became desperately ill I did not want to marry her," he explained. "But with illness, the rough edges of her personality were smoothed out. We grew comfortable and familiar, like a pair of old shoes. We converged mentally and psychologically, and there was a real level of comfort. Love developed between us as she lost her acerbic side, and we both had the sense that the end was approaching. Her death was a real loss."

Whatever the underlying dynamic, the recognition of death enabled both Niles and Esmé to find one another's sweeter side and to unite with reciprocal love. After her death, Niles arranged a beautiful funeral service that honored her and reflected the love they had found almost, but not quite, too late. It is a gift for loss to be unexpectedly postponed long enough for one to undo wrongs and seize opportunities. After more than two decades in their own strange but stable limbo, Niles and Esmé received that gift and were able to make the most of it.

In his mid-fifties, Niles expressed gentle amazement at the turn his life had taken. "I had always wanted a family and children," he said. "But I guess I was oblivious to the passage of time. It is hard to believe that more than twenty years have passed, and now I, who had never wanted to marry her, am a widower."

Retreat Is Not Always Rejection

It is not uncommon for couples living with illness (and for well couples also) to flow between being together and being apart. At different moments during the illness journey, each member of the couple—whether sick or well—may need to emotionally withdraw for a period of time to focus on his own needs. A person facing serious illness requires every ounce of emotional energy simply to put one foot in front of the other, day after day. To cope with emotional stress while at the same time working to strengthen the body to fight illness, the ill partner may need to retreat or seek support outside the couple relationship. One woman whom we interviewed did not even want to open her get-well cards, let alone focus on the needs of her family, so intent was she on recovery.

The well partner might also need to retreat into his own world, to seek support, strength, warmth, and the courage to continue from friends, family, and perhaps a counselor. The well partner may need a private space in which to engage in activities that remind him of his strengths, activities he can no longer share with his ill partner—a bike ride, a movie, a hike. While he may feel guilty about doing what his ill partner cannot do, reclaiming his own abilities can help him return to the ill partner refreshed.

For some couples, illness can create an insurmountable barrier, and the periods of retreat can far outweigh the moments of connection. For other couples dealing with illness, the balance between connection and retreat is more tolerable, and for still others the oscillation enables each partner to advance and mature. Some couples have such a secure bond that even when in retreat, they carry their connection with them.

It is important for both partners to distinguish "retreat" from "rejection" and not to take the distance personally. Like a marathon runner stepping off the track for a drink before rejoining the race, each member of a couple coping with illness needs time to retreat, regroup, and find the strength to continue the journey, together or apart.

Postscript

The duration of chronic illness can strain the bonds of intimacy. Both partners may begin to move through life in parallel, living together and performing the functions of daily life without connecting. For couples like Niles and Esmé who, for better and for worse, remained tied closely together, terminal illness can launch the relationship into surprising closeness, while exposing each partner's hidden reservoirs of resilience. Some may find, as this couple did, that illness and impending death serve as a catapult that hurls them through the toxic patterns in their relationship to new intimacy. Other couples who stay together do not necessarily find their way through the tangle of relationship issues and can wind up burdening each other with unspoken resentments, guilt, and anger. Permanent separation may result. Sometimes couples may benefit from counseling to illuminate and bring to the surface unspoken or unresolved issues that are causing problems.

Some couples find that one way to stay emotionally connected, especially when the ill partner requires care beyond the abilities of the well partner, or suffers from dementia, is to create a physical separation. Moving the ill partner to a care facility may free the well partner from the demands of daily care and create the space for him to be more emotionally present. Marian's decision to place Arthur in a nursing home allowed her to create a new equilibrium from which she could ensure Arthur's safety and comfort while giving herself the opportunity to pursue a fulfilling life. Distance made connection possible for them.

For couples to find the balance between closeness and distance that best suits their relationship, it is helpful to consider the following:

- Become aware of old patterns, outdated roles, and unproductive routines that might once have been useful but, with the addition of illness to the dynamic, now grow dysfunctional. With awareness (which at times may require therapy), the couple is better able to turn automatic, hurtful reactions into constructive choices.

- Understand that the illness is not the same for both partners. One person is experiencing the change in his body; the other is experiencing a change in the person she loves. The ill partner, in grieving the loss of function and opportunity, may need time to cry or be quiet. The well partner, trying to hold onto normal life with her beloved, may attempt to enlist him in activities and socializing. The clash between these two approaches can result in confusion and unintended distance.

- Distinguish "retreat" from "rejection," and learn not to take the need for restorative distance personally. At times during the many phases of an illness, each partner may need to retreat and regroup in order to find the strength to reconnect.

- Remember, as Dr. Shapiro affirms, "It's never too late to have a happy ending—to revisit old ghosts and put them to rest."

Whether they are together or apart, most couples—especially those in long-term relationships—are often so attuned to each other that each person subconsciously responds to the other's moods and feelings, much like violin strings that stand alone but vibrate to sound produced in neighboring strings. In the world of music, this is called "sympathetic vibration."

In negotiating closeness and distance in an illness situation, the illness itself can distort the music of the relationship and make it hard for partners to resonate with each other. As we see from the two different examples in this chapter, there is no right way to establish balance and harmony. There is only permission to experiment with a wide range of together-apart permutations in the hope of vibrating in mutual sympathy.

Chapter 5

Active Coping: Taking Charge
of Your Care and Yourself

As a culture, we have moved away from trusting in our body's wisdom to guide us towards health. Helen Battler, a spiritual care specialist, calls this wisdom "the million-year-old healer in all of us." In the first half of the 1900s, we advanced to offering that trust to an affable, grandfatherly doctor who came to our home toting his trusty black bag and drank a glass of tea before seeing the patient in her bedroom. We have now shifted that trust to a medical institution that requires us to travel to a strange building where we sit for an indeterminate amount of time surrounded by other sick people until our doctor can see us for fifteen minutes. We invest a lifetime's intimacy with our body into that narrow time slot and erase our own health intuition as soon as the doctor gives our ailment a name and recommends treatment. Even when the doctor is correct, we lose the connection to our inner wisdom and the value and sustenance it can provide. As Dr. Pierre Faubert, Jungian analyst, said, "We are addicted to the experts and need our expert fix."

Many of us have stories to tell about a doctor's diagnostic error or about treatments that were worse than the original condition. One woman we spoke with described her complaint of swollen fingers that caused pain when she flexed them. She went to a new doctor in a busy hospital clinic. After a ten-minute exam, he diagnosed psoriatic arthritis and wrote a prescription for anti-rheumatic drugs. For some reason she kept putting off filling the prescription. When asked by her husband, "Why don't you start taking the drugs?" she could only say that it didn't "sit right" with her. As she thought about it, she began to wonder if the new ointment she had begun putting on her dry, cracked feet might be affecting her hands. She had mentioned this ointment to the doctor, but he flew right by it. She stopped using the ointment and within a few days her hands returned to normal. Her inner "million-year-old healer" led her in the right direction.

This is not intended to devalue our health care system. We need it. We would not survive as well or as long as we do without it. Nor is this intended to diminish the value of what doctors and other practitioners know. They dedicate themselves to lifelong learning about their specialty areas. But there seems to be a gap between what the individual patient wants and what traditional health care provides. A recent study by the National Institutes of Health found that in the U.S., out-of-pocket spending on herbal supplements, chiropractic visits, acupuncture, meditation, and other forms of complementary and alternative medicine was estimated to be $34 billion in a single year.[2] We are looking elsewhere to find the care and relationship quality we want.

But seeking alternative help is not enough. The frailties we bring into the conventional doctor's office can easily accompany us into the treatment room of our acupuncturist or massage therapist. We can imbue the alternative practitioner with the same omniscience we attribute to our conventional specialist. We can abdicate our power and our bodily knowledge to the Reiki master just as we would to the neurologist.

In this chapter, we meet two couples who have taken charge of their health care situations. The first couple, Don and Robert, had only been together one and a half years when they had to shift quickly into active coping mode to get help for Don's sudden, mysterious kidney condition. The second couple, Abe and Betty, found themselves dealing with her diagnosis of multiple sclerosis two years after they married at the age of twenty-one. For the next thirty years, as Betty slowly declined, the couple had to actively negotiate with the health care and insurance systems that are structured more to deal with acute, episodic care rather than the long-term needs of a chronic, debilitating illness. To make matters more difficult, they also had to cope with the lost dreams and cruel realities this situation brought into their relationship.

[2] NCCAM, http://nccam.nih.gov/news/2009/073009.htm

Don and Robert: The Power of Intimacy

Don and Robert's first meeting could have been a scene from a romantic comedy. They were standing on opposite sides of a train track, waiting for trains to take them in different directions. They glanced at one another several times, but held the gaze long enough to confirm their mutual interest. Their trains arrived at the same time. Robert decided he couldn't leave without knowing if his counterpart on the other side was interested in him or not. He watched his train leave the station and then looked in the direction of Don's departing train. When he saw the last car clear the turn out of the station, he looked back toward the platform. There was Don, still on the platform, with a big smile on his face.

They dove into the process of learning about each other with hope sparked by the clever way fate brought them together, and with trepidation based on the sorrows of past failed relationships. They discovered delightful commonalities—both loved to cook, both had lived in Brazil and spoke Portuguese, both identified strongly as black men. They also found intriguing differences—Robert is an intuitive artist, and Don is an analytic businessperson.

August 2005 brought a severe test into their relationship when Hurricane Katrina destroyed Robert's childhood New Orleans home, scattered his family, and shredded his community. The support and comfort Don provided, along with Robert's vulnerability and emotional openness, propelled them into a committed relationship. Robert said, "I'm not sure how or when I knew that Don was part of the meaning of my life. I crossed some threshold and it emerged into my consciousness that he is my family. It was not a decision, but something I became aware of in hindsight." Don added that he saw their relationship "heading to forever."

Partnerships with Providers

For the first eighteen months of their relationship, neither of them even had a cold. Then, unexpectedly, Don noticed that his legs and ankles were getting increasingly bloated. Both he and Robert suspected something serious, but Don's doctors had no answers. The next five months were a horrible period of not knowing and fearing the worst. Don had to visit the emergency room twice because fluid had built up in his lungs and he had difficulty breathing. One night he passed out at the dinner table. Finally, a kidney biopsy was done and Don was diagnosed with nephrotic syndrome, damage to the filtering system in the kidneys, which, if improperly treated, could lead to renal failure.

The first phase of Don and Robert's relationship with the health care system was a typical one in which the patient is a compliant recipient of appointments, tests, medications, and instructions. Don's primary care physician referred him to a kidney specialist. They waited and waited for that appointment. Other doctors ordered additional tests and set up more appointments. They were grateful to find someone who took charge and made decisions. Waiting, not knowing, and depending on someone with the requisite white coat who is willing to engage are indications of the dependency that health care systems can foster in patients. Many people are content to remain in this space either because it suits their natures or because their conditions require nothing more. Don and Robert were not content with this passive approach—either in terms of their relationship with the health care system or with each other.

As Don and Robert learned how complicated and demanding Don's illness was, they also realized that for them to get the care Don needed they would have to take the initiative. Dr. Suzanne McCarthy, Psy.D, a researcher in the area of couples and cancer, said to us, "You need to be your advocate in the health care system. You need to take an active stance." For Don and Robert, the first step was to gather information about Don's condition and learn who had the expertise they needed. Don asserted, "I will not have a passive relationship with my doctors. I am not at the mercy of my medical team. They work for me. I am in charge. I get to make the decisions." To take responsibility for your own health is a fundamental component of active coping.

During one hospitalization, an intern was about to dispense a change in the medication Don had been taking successfully for years for another condition. Don told him, "You can't do this. I am not just a body. I insist on being in this process as a partner. This is non-negotiable. You don't just do stuff to me. Get my doctor up here." Later that day, the department head came into Don's room and thanked him. "We need to be reminded of this," he said.

Most importantly for their relationship, Don and Robert approached this illness as a team. They did separate research, compared notes, and came up with a list of questions for each doctor to address. Unfortunately, there were no clear answers. There were only options with some benefits and some side effects. They decided to seek a second opinion, even if it risked alienating Don's primary nephrologist. The second opinion helped them better understand the various treatment choices and gave them greater confidence in continuing to work with Don's original doctor. They were coping actively, and in doing so felt better able to handle the complexities of their situation.

. . . .

DR. RUTH LIPMAN — MAKING INFORMED DECISIONS

Ruth Lipman, Ph.D., a researcher at the Foundation for Informed Medical Decisions, is an expert on active coping strategies. In order for people to make informed decisions about their health care they need not only information, they need to know the questions to ask and where to get the answers.

The Internet is a great source of information, but not all sites are equally trustworthy. Dr. Lipman warns people to "be leery of ad hoc 'googling.' Many websites are underwritten by drug companies. Go to sites that are reputable, such as governmental ones. The National Institutes of Health has information about treatment options and clinical trials. Hospital-affiliated websites can also be useful." She adds, "Many health foundations are not unbiased. They too can be underwritten by drug or insurance companies. Any website you rely on should be free of advertising."

Dr. Lipman has useful parameters for assessing specialists. She emphasizes that you have to feel comfortable talking. "If you're afraid to ask questions, that's a problem." Dr. Lipman adds, "Outcomes are better if the doctor and hospital have treated people with your condition and have done a lot of what you need." She also recommends that people feel comfortable with the support staff. "You will be relying on these people a lot."

"It can be difficult for people to question the need for diagnostic tests and the efficacy of treatments." Dr. Lipman says, "People should not go unthinkingly through all screening and treatment procedures." She suggests people ask the doctor, "Why do you recommend this treatment or test? What are you hoping to gain from it? How reliable is it? What will you do with the results? What are other options?" If you don't get satisfactory answers, ask someone else. Dr. Lipman adds, "Almost always seek a second opinion. Procedures that have a higher risk warrant more opinions."

. . . .

Active coping requires that you take charge of your own health and that of your partner. Behaviorally or psychologically, responses to a challenging situation should attempt to change the threat directly or alter one's thinking about the challenge. Studies of patients with HIV, breast cancer, and other illnesses have found that active coping correlates with better quality of life and potentially with a reduction in symptoms.

Active coping behaviors typically include:

- Seeking information

- Finding social support or professional help

- Changing environments

- Reframing the meaning of the challenge

- Engaging in activities

- Solving problems

These are the manifestations of active coping. But at its root lies a painfully budding awareness of the insufficiencies of the health care system, of the fact that doctors and alternative medicine practitioners really don't know everything and are themselves searching for new knowledge, combined with the sobering realization that no one is going to organize your path through this system for you and your partner. You have to infuse yourself with vigor and courage in order to get you what you need from the health care system and in your relationship with your partner.

Debra, a healthy, forty-eight-year-old woman we met, practiced active coping. She was advised to consult with a surgeon about a lump she noticed on her abdomen. The surgeon examined her and diagnosed the lump as a "lipoma." Debra, hearing the suffix "oma," nervously asked, "What is that?" The doctor responded, "It's a benign fatty tumor." Debra relaxed a bit and said, "Well, what do you recommend for treatment?" The surgeon said, "Remove it surgically." Debra then asked, "If it's benign, why do you recommend surgery?" The doctor answered, "Because I'm a surgeon. That's what I do." Debra and her lipoma went home intact.

Accelerating Intimacy

Serious illness condenses time and space and forces the couple to focus on the present moment. Now is the time to take medication, to check blood pressure, to call for test results. Serious illness also exposes both body and emotions to a directness and urgency that many well couples never achieve. Living in the moment with physical and emotional openness and vulnerability can either swamp a couple or heighten their intimacy.

For Don and Robert, living in the crucible of illness melded them together in very intimate ways. Don said, "Illness pushed things along more aggressively. We have gained in intimacy and sharing." For a six-month period, while Don was weak and housebound, they lived together. Robert said, "Making room, sharing drawers, changing my diet to match his needs were all tangible ways in which our lives were becoming entwined." Robert became acutely tuned into what Don needed in order to feel comfortable and balanced. "I preferred to be within earshot as much as I could. I could see that this was life-threatening, and I was frustrated that I couldn't make him better. I was also terrified by having to catch him when he fainted or call an ambulance, not knowing if he was dying in my arms."

As stressful as this was, Robert appreciated that "we gained a level of intimacy we hadn't had before." Robert tried to infuse even regular medical procedures, like giving Don his injections or changing a bandage, with caring. He tried to keep them rooted in the "small things that really matter—gestures, caresses, taking time together and really listening."

The Protection Racket: To Share or Not to Share

Active coping is as much about how you behave in your relationship as it is about how you manage your health. Like many caregivers, Robert struggled with how much distress to reveal to his ill partner. Robert often felt pulled by multiple stressors. Difficulties at work, medical worries, relationship issues, and daily chores left him feeling unbalanced and exhausted. He was exasperated with the slow creep of Don's evaluation, terrified of losing him, and helpless to make him better. He began having flashbacks to a previous long-term partner who had died. Some evenings, after Don was asleep, Robert would cry silently by his side. He would wake up during the night to watch Don breathe. He kept the depth of his pain private because he was concerned that his raw emotion would overburden Don. Don learned that he had to explicitly ask Robert, "What's going on for you, really?" to move them to a deeper, more mutual exchange.

Many caregivers struggle to balance what they share and what they hide of their own stress, often leaning heavily on the side of silence. Like Robert, they fear that expressing worries and sadness will crush the partner's spirit and further overtax depleted coping resources. They fear that their feelings, once expressed, will make the partner sicker and that being "strong" through silence will somehow strengthen the partner.

Ironically, this approach can have the exact opposite effect. The ill partner, in all likelihood, suspects or senses that the well partner is experiencing emotional distress. When the well partner hides this distress, the ill partner consciously or subconsciously might assume that the well partner is protecting himself and colludes in concealing the well partner's suffering. This has two possible effects. It can insert an emotional no-fly-zone in between the partners and leave each partner feeling more isolated from the other. The well partner may not only lose the life he constructed with his partner but may also lose the full presence of his primary emotional support.

In addition, the ill partner, most likely, has had his identity as a contributing, high-functioning adult turned into that of the patient, dependent and fragile. When the well partner conceals his distress, he cheats the ill partner of a vital opportunity to minister, to be the one offering solace, and to remember, and even reclaim, an area of competence. Bonnie, a thirty-two-year-old woman with lupus who has lived with debilitating symptoms for many years, described to us the moment when her partner broke down sobbing in her arms. For the first time in years, she felt strong and able to "give a little bit back to him of what he has so selflessly given me: comfort."

It wasn't only Robert who struggled with this issue. Don didn't want to "dump all his stuff" on Robert, especially given that their relationship was still relatively new, and he didn't yet know how resilient it was. One night, over dinner, Don was unusually quiet, engaged in an internal debate about whether he should share his fears with Robert. The pressure built to the point where words just spilled from his mouth. He finally said, "This is so hard for me," and began crying. Instead of scaring Robert away, this emotional release brought him closer to Don.

Don then began asking Robert to share his feelings, and they both became more open about expressing emotion. Don said to Robert, "Whatever this path is that we're on, it will be a journey, and if we want to stay in touch with each other it will be important for us to share our feelings along the way."

In addition to Robert helping Don advocate for his medical needs, he acted as "ballast" for Don's emotional swings. When Don got emotionally whiplashed by lab test results that indicated remission one day and exacerbation a week later, or by contradictory advice from different doctors, or by the appearance of a new symptom, or when he felt held hostage to the demands of the illness, he easily slid to the dark side and assumed the worst. Robert balanced his darkness with patience and hope. Robert would say, "Just breathe. We don't know what this means so let's not jump to conclusions. Let's be vigilant and curious." This not only allowed Don to move more powerfully into his feelings and take the risk of not holding back, it also permitted him to engage with his sense of his own mortality. He started to let go of the physical person he used to be and to expand into the fullness of his essential self. Don became acutely aware of time and mortality, and he began paring away what was non-essential, while deepening his friendships with the people he loved. He also talked openly with Robert about his will and asked him to be his health care proxy.

The Relationship: A Cradle of Respite

The relational aspect of active coping is often overlooked by researchers, who tend to focus on the patient's individual behaviors. However, a profound aspect of active coping is to be found in the dynamics of the couple's relationship. The relationship can become the cradle in which the couple finds respite from the abuses of illness. For some couples, it can hold them with tenderness and sweetly rock them until they are returned to their essence, which is love and wholeness. The relationship can fortify them and give each person a partner to accompany him in dealing with the illness. For some couples, the relationship has grown too toxic over the years and can never be a place of sanctuary. For some, the pre-illness relationship is on autopilot, carrying them through repetitive daily activities, with periodic excursions to authentic connecting. For those whose relationship still has nurturing potential, to create this cradle and find that place of peace and partnership requires focus and effort. For a couple to consciously orchestrate their relationship and turn it into their sanctuary, as Don and Robert have, is one of the most powerful forms of active coping.

Abe and Betty: The Long Haul

Abe and Betty met when they were undergraduates and lived in the same cooperative housing. Abe had experienced little success in previous relationships and was swept away when Betty took the initiative. Abe said, "When she seduced me, that was it!" They were both twenty years old at the time, and became inseparable. They moved together to an off-campus apartment. When Betty had to relocate to attend nursing school in another state, there was no question that Abe would join her. They married when they were both twenty-three.

Their relationship had all the hallmarks of young love: romantic walks, intellectual communion, private jokes, and lots of sex. This cozy marital cocoon kept them sheltered for two years. Then Betty developed her first symptom, tightness around the abdomen. A friend who was a nurse in a neurology clinic recommended a full work-up.

Abe remembered holding Betty's hand as she lay in a hospital bed during the testing procedures. The routine clamor of the hospital corridors was overpowered by the voice of a sports commentator coming from the black-and-white TV in the corner of the room. Abe gave Betty's hand an encouraging squeeze as it was announced that the 1980 U.S. Olympic hockey team had upset the Russians and went on to win the gold medal—as if their victory could somehow translate into triumph for Betty.

Betty was diagnosed with multiple sclerosis, about which much less was known in 1980. The doctor told them that there were three kinds of MS: only one symptomatic episode; a series of exacerbations followed by remissions; or exacerbations and continuous degeneration. The doctor could not tell which kind she had, nor could he offer Betty any viable treatment options. The couple felt as if they had been dropped from a great height into a tiny pool of dark water. They were left stunned and flailing in that dreadful realm all too familiar to people living with a chronic degenerative illness: the realm of not knowing.

The Torment of Uncertainty

Healthy people live with not knowing, and do so in a state of comfortable ignorance. They do not have to weigh every activity against its physical consequences. Often, they are not even aware of time; whereas ill people, especially if pain is involved, know exactly how many minutes separate them from their next medication dose.

However, a particularly tormenting type of not knowing accompanies progressive illness in which the pattern is unpredictable, the degree of debilitation is erratic, and only the final outcome is assured. If completely denied, this form of not knowing can lead to chaos; if fully acknowledged, it can lead to emotional overload. The toll this takes on the ill partner is fierce. The effect on the well partner—who in addition to monitoring his own anxiety must also take care of the ill partner, the children, and his job—can be damaging. How can either partner come through safer, and even stronger? Don and Robert achieved this. For Abe and Betty, it was more difficult.

For years, Betty's course was stably unstable. She could count on having four to five exacerbations of her MS symptoms each year. These episodes would resolve, but each remission left her less functional, and over time, each episode took longer to resolve. Initially, the flare-ups lasted a few weeks, then a month, then a few months. During their initial phase of learning about MS, Betty and Abe carried out intensive research, especially about alternative approaches such as gluten-free diets, B vitamins, and homeopathy. However, as Abe said, "With this disease nothing is immediate. You try something, and you just don't know the result. The relationship between cause and effect is impossible to figure out. You have no clue if the treatment you tried was successful, or produced another episode, or had no impact." Each remission raised hopes that something was finally working. But each exacerbation dropped Abe and Betty back into that pool of dark water.

Betty's Way: Becoming Her Illness

Before her illness, Betty had been a strong hiker, an imaginative cook, an organic gardener, and a talented artist. She was rarely without a project in which to immerse herself. Knitting yarn, plant shoots, recipes, and paint tubes littered most of the surfaces in their house. Her conversations took place while her hands were occupied with a spatula, trowel, or paintbrush. Her sense of herself was rooted not in an inner identity, but rather in activities.

Betty coped with MS by immersing herself in her disease as she had once done with her projects. She hungrily read medical texts and journals and articles on alternative healing. As she became more debilitated by muscle weakness, poor coordination, numbness, incontinence, and speech difficulties, she extended her research to include home adaptations, equipment, and insurance-covered services. Abe felt that her absorption in her illness left little room for empathy for him. What extra energy she had she focused on their two young children. Her sense of self, once dependent on her talents, now became fused with her illness.

Like many others who live with all the unknowns of a chronic, degenerative disease, Betty tried to gain a sense of control over her failing body by identifying with the agent that was consuming it, her MS, and trying to overpower it with information. While research can be an active coping tool, Betty was really using it as her primary defense against illness. Sadly, this left Betty more constricted and isolated, and limited her to a realm occupied only by herself and her illness.

Dr. Pierre Faubert, a Jungian analyst, said, "You can die sick, but you can also die healed—healed spiritually, psychologically, emotionally." With her exclusive connection to her illness, Betty was on a path to dying sick. Dr. Faubert explained that you can be in communion with a deeper part of yourself, the part that connects you to your soul, to the divine, to the universe, and activate that part to work on behalf of your entire self. As you reclaim more of your authentic, inner self and allow your true voice to speak on your behalf, you will be better able to see where you need to go and have more inner strength to get there.

Abe's Way: Releasing the Emotion

Sometimes it's easier to cope with one whopping crisis than it is to deal with the incremental accumulation of inconvenience. A crisis can shift us into action and heroism, while mounting inconveniences can cause exasperation and defeat. We can mobilize for a midnight rush to the hospital, but a missing shirt button or a zipper that sticks can drive us mad. For Abe, it was a shoe.

Abe's upbringing had taught him that the man is supposed to "do it all" for the family: to provide materially and emotionally in as stoic and ceaseless a way as is humanly possible. Abe tried hard to live up to this model. Betty was wheelchair-bound by the time their younger child was one and their older child was four. Abe not only had to help Betty with bathing, toileting, eating, and taking medication; he also had to attend to the interminable needs of two inventive, agile young children.

Abe recalled one morning when, after a sleepless night during which he had to help Betty to the commode four times, he prepared breakfast for the children, helped them brush their teeth and get dressed, and drove them to school. Then he returned home to help Betty get out of bed, wash, and dress, while being acutely aware that he was becoming increasingly late for work and that there was no way to hurry Betty along. After he had situated her in the wheelchair he reached for her right shoe. Her spasticity made it hard for her to flex her ankle to ease her foot into the shoe. Abe struggled to get the right angle, but her foot would not slide into that shoe. He tried again and again, realizing that he was now an hour late for work.

In frustration, he threw the shoe aside and burst into tears, suddenly overcome by desperate loneliness and bleakness. "I felt so forlorn and dismal," he said. Abe had always been able to "make it work." He had put handrails in the bathroom and had widened doorways to accommodate Betty's wheelchair, but now he found himself thinking, "How the hell am I going to deal with all this?" He said, "I knew Betty wasn't going to be much help in figuring things out. Her energy was expended on what normal people don't think twice about. It really hit me how alone I was in dealing with all these challenges."

Abe began participating in a form of peer-to-peer counseling in which two people alternate listening deeply to each other in order to facilitate an emotional discharge that is intended to free each person from rigid patterns of behavior and feeling. The purpose is to leave each person better able to access his or her intellect, energy, and loving-kindness. Abe knew that he couldn't change the illness, but he hoped he could fix the issues that surrounded the illness. Initially, Abe needed a way to resolve his overwhelming sense of aloneness.

The Final Straw

Through counseling, Abe not only found empathy and support, he also found himself. He had been submerged in his wife's and his children's needs for so long, he could barely recognize his own basic requirements for sleep and food, let alone his emotional needs. This negation of self was punctuated by rare outbursts of anger, the inevitable spillover of too much numbing sacrifice.

Abe recalled one evening, after he had fed the children and put them to bed, when Betty complained about one of her daytime caregivers. Abe suddenly felt as if he were being sucked into a vortex. The dirty laundry on the floor, Betty's tray of medications, the hospital bed with its rumpled linen, her tight hands resting on the padded arms of her wheelchair, her face—all began to swirl and recede. His only anchor was his howl of rage. He shouted, "You have no clue what I am dealing with. Can't you make the slightest attempt in my direction? Can't you do anything that is good for me?"

. . . .

HELEN BATTLER — EMPTYING YOUR CUP

Helen Battler, M. Div., a spiritual care specialist, says that from the moment of diagnosis each partner embarks on a different journey. "One person is in the role of patient and the other is in the role of caregiver. These roles represent two different sets of needs, and the partners' capacity to meet each other's new needs is challenged." In addition, partners who were used to sharing may now find that they protect each other and try to hide aspects of their experience from each other. Ms. Battler says, "The ill partner will hide his deepest fears, and the well partner will hide the difficulties of being a caregiver." This gap widens just when the partners need each other's presence most.

Ms. Battler has evolved an approach to help couples in this stuation find points of connection. She calls this practice "emptying your cup." It provides a structured way for couples to come together periodically and report on their separate journeys.

1. One partner sits quietly with eyes closed and deeply listens, without commenting, to the other partner share from his heart (empty his cup).

2. When the sharing partner becomes quiet, the listening partner asks, "Is there anything more?" This invitation to look deeper and share what lies underneath the first tier of thoughts usually elicits "the real stuff."

3. Once the sharing partner has finished, they switch roles. The new sharing partner does not respond to what has just been said. She speaks about her own experience with truth and heart.

"This practice can keep the couple connected," Ms. Battler says. "Presence alone is such a powerful medicine. If someone is present to you in a moment of pain, it changes the pain."

. . . .

The Forbidden Whispers

Through counseling, Abe was invited to acknowledge his experience and express his deepest emotions. In the safety of the co-counseling relationship Abe could both shout aloud and whisper to himself. He could say, "I am angry at Betty for having MS. I hate her! I hate having to live this life!" While it might not seem like active coping, getting in touch with suppressed feelings and being able to master them instead of having them master you is indeed active coping.

There are dangers in hidden emotions. One elderly couple we spoke to, Fred and Lillian, barely had a feeling word in their vocabularies and had not expressed emotion to each other in more than fifty years. When, at age eighty-two, Fred became incapacitated by a series of falls, Lillian grew increasingly resentful of his inability to take care of activities that had always been his domain—financial investments, bill paying, and household repairs. Instead of talking about her feelings she became passive-aggressive and forgot to give him his medications on time and served him food she knew he did not like. Deeply frustrated by his inability to control his bodily functions and unable to name and express his feelings, Fred compensated by becoming increasingly controlling. He barked at Lillian to go see if the mail had arrived, to get his prescriptions renewed, and to make sure the emergency brake was released before she drove the car. In response to Fred's attempts to control her, Lillian became even more passive-aggressive and inattentive. Fred, in turn, increased his efforts to control her. They were locked into a ruthless zero-sum game that left both of them depleted and alone.

Unlike Fred and Lillian, who never expressed emotion directly, Abe chose a different approach. Initially, Abe had feared that putting his rage and his fears into words would make him seem contemptible, if not crazy. However, by expressing these outlawed feelings and having them heard and understood by his co-counselor, he became larger than them. He learned to see beyond his feelings and his current situation to appreciate that "I am not my challenges. I am bigger than the identity of being the partner of a handicapped woman. The world is OK and I am OK." He could return to Betty and, having discharged his anger, approach her with a remembrance of the young love they once shared and a renewed appreciation for the love he still carried.

This expansiveness helped him to return to his day-to-day life feeling more grounded and truthful, and knowing that there were people who could understand

and uplift him a phone call away. As Abe came to accept the full spectrum of his emotions and to gain higher insights about his situation, he was also able to reach out to his community in a forthright way.

In a letter Abe sent to his close friends and relatives, he described his situation in this way:

I struggle mightily with the fact that as I continue to be the primary caregiver to Betty, I become less able to be an emotional support to her. As I have spoken to various people over the past year about this paradox, they have shared with me various anecdotes about the situation. My favorite one, that seems to get to the core of the issue, is from a friend. She related to me that when she and her husband were planning on having her cancer-stricken mother-in-law move in with them, the doctor told her: "There are many people who can do the caretaking of your mother well. There are very few people who can do the love thing with your mother well. You can't do them both, so get someone to do the caretaking so that you can do the loving." Though I am sorry to say it, and wish it were otherwise, unhappily I have found out that this is all too true. As my caretaking responsibilities have gone on and increased, I have found myself less and less able to be a supportive, caring, and loving husband. In fact the situation is such that I experience self-loathing because I am unable to both care for Betty and treat her as well as I would like and as she deserves. To put it bluntly, I'm burnt out and my attitude stinks! And I truly want this situation to change.

Handicapped Oppression

By connecting with others in similar situations and continuing to work on expanding his own awareness, Abe also came to appreciate the impact of what he called "handicapped oppression." In the same letter he described this as severe isolation:

It is clear to me that people care about us and our well-being. However, it is rare that we get invited to do things with other families, or asked if someone can help out. I think it is fair to say that most people tend to avoid individuals who appear to have more permanent disabilities. It makes them feel that they are unwanted and undesirable, that their disability defines them and hides their otherwise "normal" humanness. As a result of this we end up feeling that the disability defines us and is not just something that unfortunately happened to us. We are for all intents and purposes as "normal" as anyone else, with the same desire for closeness and involvement with other people and their lives.

What About Intimacy?

By the mid-1990s, Betty's MS had gone into steady decline. She needed constant care and could not be left alone. Her physical limitations increased, and it soon became apparent that her cognitive functioning was impaired. She was diagnosed with early-onset dementia. Ironically, the fact that Betty had cognitive losses and couldn't process information and experience coherently made it easier for Abe to be kinder and more loving. He could accept that her lack of empathy for him and inability to connect with him were not intentional.

Not for a moment did Abe consider leaving Betty. But through counseling, he had come to an undeniable realization that his life had revolved around caretaking for almost thirty years, and he did not want to be only a caretaker for his entire life. He wanted intimacy. Abe recognized that "I could be okay with being married and pursuing a sexual relationship with someone else just to sustain me."

Well partners in the situation of being the primary caretaker for someone who is no longer able or interested in engaging in sexual relations eventually wrestle with the issue of intimacy. Some accept that sex is no longer a part of their lives. Some discover that there are ways to be sexual with their partner that don't involve intercourse. Some successfully suppress their own desires, and some cannot. Dissatisfaction may seep into the primary relationship in distorted ways as misplaced rage, distance, or even neglect. Some well partners seek companionship and sex outside the primary relationship. This last course was the one Abe chose.

Initially, he approached women he knew and openly told them of his home situation and explained that he was looking for someone to be sexual with occasionally. While the women he asked were understanding, even sweet, no one accepted his invitation.

Finally, he did meet a woman with whom he unexpectedly fell in love. Abe was honest with her about his situation, and she remained interested in getting to know him. Abe soon realized that this was not going to be a casual relationship.

He decided to tell Betty about this woman in order to see if there were a way to incorporate this relationship into their family. They lived in an area in which non-traditional families were common, so the concept was not radical. However, the attempts to assimilate this new relationship were not successful.

Abe continued to be involved with this woman and after two years, they knew that they would be life partners. While this new relationship brought intimacy into his life, it also increased the complexity of his situation. He now had even more to juggle and began to feel a dangerous degree of stress.

Abe had been diagnosed with a heart condition ten years earlier, atrial fibrillation, and had two or three episodes of abnormal heart rhythm a year. A year after he began his new relationship, the episodes increased. His doctors told him that stress was a major contributing factor, and Abe saw his increasing caretaking load as his most significant source of stress.

With great difficulty, Abe decided that Betty would have to go to a nursing home. He believed that if she remained at home, he could become very ill and perhaps die. The better option, although an infinitely sad one, was to have Betty taken care of in a nearby nursing home and have Abe remain as healthy as possible. Betty, lucid for the first time in a long while, responded by saying, "I feel like I'm being thrown out of my home." Clearly, moving to a nursing home was not her choice, but as often happens with people suffering from degenerative physical and mental illness, her sphere of autonomy decreased as her disability increased.

Abe took no action for six months. The family spent the time crying and in counseling. Their younger daughter, by this time a college graduate, summed up the situation: "This really sucks. But it's just the newest version of suckiness." Finally, Abe transitioned Betty to an excellent nursing home. Abe visited Betty in the nursing home several times a week. He continued to find connection and intimacy in his new relationship.

Did Abe Really Use Active Coping?

During the long haul of Betty's degenerative illness, Abe used active coping in the text-book way. He researched her condition thoroughly. He went to doctor and alternative practitioner visits with Betty and did not shy away from asking tough questions. In addition he researched care resources, sought out and interviewed aides, applied for available insurance and disability funds, made their house completely accessible, and tried to keep Betty engaged with their community.

Abe also used active coping by entering into counseling. For over twenty-five years he committed to exploring his motivations, patterns, old wounds, and buried emotions. He wanted to be as honest with himself as he could and as pure in his actions as self-awareness could make him. He could not change the illness, but he could, and did, change himself and his life. He strengthened the psychological musculature he needed to deal with his challenges.

For Abe, the choices to seek a partner outside of marriage and to eventually place his wife in a nursing home were acts of active coping. While his choices may arouse negative judgment for some, long-term, degenerative illness does not come with an instruction booklet. Abe made difficult decisions in a miserable situation, and he did so with what he considered to be the best interests of all in mind.

Postscript

It would be comforting to believe that through active coping, couples get the attention they need from the health care system and find a higher path to building a stronger relationship. The truth is, some do and some don't. And some do for periods of time, often depending on the course of the illness. However, active coping—being informed about the illness, building a partnership with your providers, and being clear about your relationship needs—is usually a better option than being a passive, uninformed participant, both in the health care system and the couple relationship. To cope actively with your illness situation:

- Solve problems, seek information, find social support or professional help, change environments, reframe the meaning of the challenge, engage in activities.

- Be your own advocate and case manager in the health care system. As Don asserted, "I will not have a passive relationship with my doctors. I am not at the mercy of my medical team. They work for me. I am in charge. I get to make the decisions."

- Become knowledgeable about the illness. Use the Internet cautiously: many health information websites have a bias. Use government and hospital-affiliated sites.

- Find health care providers who have the expertise you need, ones who have treated many people with your condition.

- Ask questions about the need for diagnostic tests, as well as the efficacy of treatments. "Why do you recommend this treatment or test? What are you hoping to gain from it? How reliable is it? What will you do with the results? What other options exist?"

- Dr. Lipman advises, "Almost always seek a second opinion. Procedures that have a higher risk warrant more opinions."

- Strengthen your relationship through communication and compassion. The relationship can fortify partners and become a shelter from the assaults of the illness and frustrations with the health care system.

- Share your feelings about your hardships with your partner. The ill partner tends to conceal his deepest fears, and the well partner tends to diminish the difficulties of being a caretaker. The distance this benevolent deception causes increases just at the time when partners need one another most.

- Use counseling when necessary. You may find not only empathy and support, but also attributes of yourself that can become a source of strength to you and your partner.

- Know that healing is always possible, even in desperate illness situations. Dr. Pierre Faubert tells us, "You can die sick, but you can also die healed—healed spiritually, psychologically, emotionally." To pursue healing, even after the body has surrendered, is perhaps the highest form of active coping.

Active coping is not easy. It takes courage and insight to declare your needs to be as important as those of your doctors and your partner. It takes greater courage to penetrate your own defenses and express the feelings and insights concealed inside. It takes still greater courage to develop true empathy for the experience of your partner and hold his hand while you suffer his sorrows along with your own. But it takes the greatest courage of all to make painful decisions, the kind that serious illness can force upon us: decisions to put your beloved in a facility, to give your well partner permission to exit the relationship, to undertake drastic medical measures and undergo risky clinical trials, to stop treatment, to end life—and, most importantly, to live with the aftermath. If we face illness with this kind of courage, with this active coping, even if we are unable to influence the path of the illness, we will surely become more of who we can be. And we, ill and well partner, get to carry that greater self into the future.

Chapter 6

Standing Together:
The Circle of Community

C ouples do not live in isolation, either before or after illness. Typically they are
part of a social network that includes their family members, friends, colleagues,
coworkers, health care providers, and others. This network can be large, even global, or
it can be tight and bounded by kinship. We have explored how illness in one partner
deeply affects the couple relationship. Further, illness in the couple relationship reverberates throughout their social network. Close friends and relatives will be most affected; those on the periphery will take note but carry on with their daily lives. In addition,
illness thrusts the couple into contact with new networks, primarily the health care system and the providers who care for the ill partner. All these networks, when activated
and aligned, form a powerful circle of community around the couple, providing them
with practical and emotional reinforcement. In this chapter we explore advice for how
each couple can build and draw strength from a community of support.

The Strength of Community

The primary community that surrounds the couple, made up of friends and family, can
carry the couple from one moment to another: from fear to comfort, from isolation
to fellowship. The community accompanies the couple as they wend their way from

hope to sorrow, sorrow to hope. The constant presence of love and sympathy become arms that the couple can lean into when they need support. For Frances, whom we met in Chapter 3, the community carried hope when her pain expanded to occupy all the space inside her body, and she had no awareness of anything beyond. Her friends and family reminded her that she would get better, even though she could not yet imagine a life without pain.

Community members play three important roles for the couple: they organize, they act, and they support. Often there are a few people in the community who take it upon themselves to organize initiatives on behalf of the couple. Nancy, who had lymphoma (a cancer of the immune system), had a close friend who arranged dozens of bone marrow donor drives. Another friend used a website to create a calendar of chores that needed to be done, and invited the rest of the community to sign up online. These organizers built the scaffolding that held the couple steady.

Other community members act. They take on chores, cook food, babysit children, drive the ill partner to medical appointments, get prescriptions refilled, take the well partner out to a ball game, and more.

When Bonnie, a mother of two school-aged children, was diagnosed with breast cancer and endured exhausting chemotherapy, the local PTA (Parent Teacher Association) sprang into action. Working from a master schedule, the PTA president collected names of neighbors who wanted to help and assigned each family a task: deliver dinner to the family of the ill woman; ferry the children to after-school activities or have them for sleepovers to give Mom and Dad a break and some time alone. This went on for weeks until the chemo was completed and Bonnie was back on her feet. "So much food was delivered to our house, including a full turkey dinner with all the trimmings, that we had to buy a second refrigerator to keep in the basement," said Bonnie. Added her husband, "At a time when I felt most alone and burdened by family responsibilities, it was important to know that we had the support of our community."

Other community members provide emotional support. They leave voicemails or send emails letting the couple know that they are thinking of them. They listen deeply and empathize. They are sensitive to the couple's needs and know when to approach and when to sit quietly. When the couple needs to be distracted from the weight of illness, friends and relatives tell stories, reminisce, read aloud from a book, or download a movie. Should the ill partner want to cry over her losses or talk about how she wants to die, these community members are unwaveringly present. They hold the well partner when he finally releases the sorrow he has kept hidden from his partner. And they also support other community members, check in with those who seem worried or fragile, and initiate conversations with other community members to make sure they are not becoming overwhelmed by emotion or tasks. This kind of community support is in stark contrast to the isolation described by Abe in Chapter 5.

How to Construct a Helping Community

The good news is that your community already exists. You don't have to go out and recruit members. In fact, your community is probably larger than you imagine and can consist not only of the friends and relatives you have regular contact with, but also people who belong to the same organizations as you (the PTA, a church or synagogue or mosque, your workplace).

While your community doesn't have to be created, it does need to be organized. People want to help but also appreciate guidance. The couple should make their needs and their boundaries clear to the key members of the community, particularly the "leaders." The couple can list the areas in which they need tangible help and provide instructions where necessary. Nancy, who had lymphoma, did not have the energy to prepare meals. To complicate matters, her husband, Joel, had severe dietary restrictions due to food allergies. Joel provided their community with a list of acceptable foods, possible menus, and safe takeout restaurants. Initially he was worried that he was overburdening his friends and family. Several friends, however, told him that they were relieved to be able to help, guided by detailed instructions that enabled them to carry out their tasks with confidence.

The couple should also be explicit about the degree of contact they want to have with others. They may want anyone to drop in any time, or they may only want to have scheduled visits with their closest friends and relatives. Most in the community, however, will want to know how both partners are doing. If the couple does not want to be swamped with emails and phone calls, they can designate someone as the communication link—someone who will provide regular updates to the rest of the community. This can be done through a weekly (or daily) email or phone tree.

As the ill partner's health status changes, the community will need to re-align itself to accommodate these changes. For example, if the ill partner improves and wants to become more active, community members may need to do less laundry on her behalf and begin taking her out for walks in the park. When Nancy had a good day, she asked her close women friends to take her out for a pancake breakfast. Should the ill partner's health decline, the community members will have to adjust their expectations and their activities. The community should also be alert to the well partner's state and respond if he needs more active support. It is especially important, under changing circumstances, for the couple to reset their social boundaries and let the community know what kind of contact they want and what new chores will be appreciated.

The Love of a Good Pet

Pets are part of your community too. They rarely get acknowledged for their extraordinary love and presence. Your dog or cat or rabbit or bird has innate powers to pull you out of despair and into the moment. One woman we spoke with wrote about her experience of having a neuropathic pain condition and a dog:

Over the next few weeks, as my pain level fluctuated, my dog Mina began to show her true powers. She proved herself to be a gifted empath who could modulate her responses to my state. When I sat quietly to meditate, she moved a few feet away, staying in range, but not intruding. When pain or depression forced me to lie down, she snuggled closely, sometimes resting her head on my shoulder.

One late afternoon, after I had been swimming in deeper and deeper pools of pain all day, I finally collapsed to the floor in a wretched heap of tears. My husband was at a loss as to how to help me. He was afraid that this time, I might have sunk too far down and would not be able to pull myself out as I had so many times before. I could see the fear in his eyes, and that only increased my sense of hopelessness.

At that moment, Mina came over and sat in the curve of my body and relaxed against me. No hugs, no licks, no attempts to persuade me to shake myself out of this state. She just rested against me, composed and patient. In her stillness, she was able to tap into that solitary, slender thread of hope that still endured somewhere deep inside me. Her calmness reassured me as no human intervention could have.

A Message for Health Care Providers

Health care providers involved in treating the ill partner rarely think of themselves as part of a helping community. They tend to work largely within their own discipline in their own clinics and to communicate with other involved providers through a medical record. Yet, for the couple, their network of providers is indeed a core community that is as fundamental to the couple's sense of safety and continuity as are their closest relatives and friends.

While health care institutions may silo their clinicians by practice area, the couple doesn't deposit their providers in separate boxes after the appointment is over. The couple holds onto the providers' counsel and experiences their interventions as part of the whole fabric that is wrapped around them. The couple may see an endocrinologist to treat the ill partner's diabetes. However, if other problems begin, they may also see an ophthalmologist, a dietician, and a podiatrist. For the couple, these clinicians represent a team, a community of care. The couple looks to them for comprehensive, integrated, timely expertise. Some facilities are organized to provide this kind of care. Many others are not. And few are positioned to incorporate the findings and interventions of alternative health care providers whom the couple may also be consulting.

How Can Clinicians Act as a Community of Care?

Unfortunately, the answer is often: with great difficulty. Reimbursement systems, clinical training, decreasing numbers of primary care doctors, and many other factors are severe impediments to building a community of care from a disaggregated collection of individual practitioners. However, there are things individual practitioners can do to provide their patients with an experience of consistency and care, even if their only contact with other involved clinicians is through the patient's medical record.

- **Access:** Patients and their partners, especially in the early crisis stage, need rapid access to primary care doctors and specialists, often in the form of an office visit. Sometimes a phone call or a response to an email will suffice. One ill partner exchanged brief emails with her primary care doctor on Friday afternoons "to carry me across the 'weekend desert,' the time when none of my clinicians is available and the only recourse is to go to a hospital emergency room." The toll that waiting takes on the patient and her partner should not be underestimated.

- **Time:** When the ill partner has a scheduled appointment, the clinician should spend the right amount of time with the couple. The amount of time that is right is derived by combining the time the clinician needs to do her job with the time the couple needs to feel heard and to fully understand her evaluation and treatment recommendations. One couple who had to wait two hours before being called in to see a specialist for a scheduled appointment said that they didn't mind waiting at all. "If she spends that much time with someone else, she'll spend whatever time is necessary with me."

- **Expertise:** The couple needs to have confidence that the clinicians who are treating the ill partner are experts. For clinicians to convey their expertise, in addition to diagnosing and prescribing, they need to build a trusting relationship with the couple, not just the ill partner. Expertise is conveyed through the conduit of that trust. If the trust is absent or damaged, the couple's appreciation of the clinician's talent will be contaminated. Building this relationship does not need to be time consuming. In the initial meetings, in which the foundation for trust is laid, the clinician needs to combine dispensing information with active listening; nonverbal connective interactions (greeting the patient while he is still dressed, eye contact with patient and partner, touching the hand); asking questions about the life impact of the illness (not just its symptomatic manifestations); providing appropriate reassurance not just about outcome, but also about the clinician's commitment to helping the patient and partner over the long haul; showing humility in terms of not being able to predict the exact course of the illness and the outcome (even in serious situations); and sustaining hope wherever it can grow—for a cure, pain control, treatment options, more time. The clinician can also arrange for support services that enable the patient to remain at home, which may be the patient's final wish. The clinician needs to be mindful of the role the partner plays in the patient's illness and healing, and should build a relationship with the partner, too. The clinician can ask the patient's permission to invite the partner into the examination room. At some point during the session, the clinician should turn to the partner and ask how he is doing. One overburdened husband told us he burst into tears when a doctor asked him that question. No one had seemed to care before.

Couples and Clinicians

The couple can play a role in supporting their clinical "community." They can be completely honest with their providers, and they can respect the providers' time. By being clear about old and new symptoms, medication compliance, medication side effects, pain levels, and emotional state, the couple is giving the clinician essential data from which the clinician can modify treatment recommendations. Without this information, the clinician is working with a distorted picture, and interventions based on distortions will be ineffective. The well partner can play a crucial role in remembering, validating, and amending the patient's version of her illness history.

The couple should demonstrate respect for the clinician's time by preparing for the appointment, arriving on time, and getting (and understanding) the information they need during the visit. Preparing for the visit includes bringing a list of issues and questions they would like to cover, along with lab test results and evaluations the clinician may not have access to. Betsy, who had chronic fatigue syndrome and a lengthy history of treatments, medications, even different diagnoses, kept a notebook that she brought to all appointments that contained her version of her illness history and copies of all lab results and clinician evaluations. One specialist told her that she had never seen such a thorough history and wanted to use it as a model for her residents. It is also important that the couple be sure that at least one of them completely understands (and has written down) the clinician's assessment and recommendations. It is likely that one partner is highly stressed and not absorbing every detail. A great advantage of having both partners in the room is that there are two questioners and two memories being applied, and what one partner doesn't recall, the other will.

Postscript

The African proverb, "It takes a village to raise a child," ignites our awareness that no one, especially not the weakest among us, can stand alone and survive, much less thrive. Couples living with illness, however, need more than a village. They need a commonwealth; a federation of villages and communities that can be rapidly activated to recognize the couple's needs and provide them with practical, emotional, and professional support as their situation changes, often in unpredictable ways. This commonwealth includes friends, relatives, and health care providers, as well as the workplace, community services, and religious institutions. Members of the commonwealth provide the couple not only with meals and clean laundry, but also, and perhaps more importantly, with a sense that they are never standing alone—that they matter and are loved.

Serious illness can break a couple apart. Some couples re-form in stronger ways, others dissipate. The commonwealth, the community of all the communities that surround the couple, can hold the broken couple and infuse them with strength and hope. The caring power of the commonwealth can carry the couple when their stamina is dangerously low, and help raise their spirits when they feel their courage depleted by the relentlessness of their ordeal.

Chapter 7

Military Couples:

Wounded Warriors Back Home

Whatever your opinions are about the wars in Iraq and Afghanistan, they don't alter the fact that over a million young men and women have been deployed and tens of thousands of them have returned severely wounded. Health problems are mounting in the fighting force and in returning veterans. According to a report from the Department of Defense Task Force on Mental Health, between 28 and 47 percent of soldiers and members of the National Guard returning from Iraq and Afghanistan suffer from post-traumatic stress disorder (PTSD) or other difficulties, such as drug and alcohol abuse, depression, anxiety, insomnia, suicidal thoughts, or additional violence against self and others.[3]

In addition to emotional injury, here are some facts about war-related physical injuries:[4]

- More American soldiers have suffered non-mortal wounds in Iraq and Afghanistan than in any other combat situation in U.S. history.

- There is a ratio of sixteen wounded servicemen for every fatality.

- Of the over 1.6 million troops deployed, more than 40,000 have returned wounded.

---

[3] US Department of Veterans Affairs, "Veterans Get Nearly $81 Billion in Historic FY 07 Plan." Public and Intergovernmental Affairs, February 5, 2006.
[4] Wikipedia, http://en.wikipedia.org/wiki/Casualties_of_the_Iraq_War

- These wounds include limb amputations, burn injuries, gastrointestinal problems, spinal cord injuries, traumatic brain injury, hearing loss, respiratory disorders, and psychiatric problems.

- Veterans between the ages of 20 and 24 are most likely to commit suicide—at a rate three times that of civilians the same age.

The soldier may suffer the effects of war in his or her body and mind, but the soldier's partner is also affected by the intrusion of the consequences of war into their relationship. While the military does provide services for returning soldiers and their families, the suffering of these families remains invisible to the general public. In this chapter we tell the story of the wife of a soldier who was deployed to Iraq and Afghanistan five times. Our expert is Kathy Platoni, Psy.D., a clinical psychologist and Army psychologist who is a colonel and not only treats psychologically wounded veterans and their families when they return home, but also accompanies troops on combat missions to the front lines in war zones. She has been deployed four times and had just returned from a year in Afghanistan when we spoke to her.

We dedicate a chapter to military couples because we feel a special responsibility to elevate their experience to a higher level of public awareness. One army nurse we spoke to said, "Sometimes the silence is indeed deafening about what happens to *all* who serve. No one comes out of the service unscathed." We believe that if our government engages in war, it is our duty to look its human consequences in the face and to listen to the voices of the wounded—soldiers, partners, and helpers. Our hope is that in hearing their voices, we will not only become advocates for improving the services they rely upon, but that we might also become more sensitized to the whole family suffering that results from sending our youth into battle. In addition, military couples have a lot to teach us about finding strength in relationships to deal with the upheavals of illness.

Pam and Doug: The Wounded Couple

"Others just don't understand what we go through day to day," said Pam as she readied herself to tell the story of her relationship with her husband Doug, who had eventually come home after five tours of duty in Iraq and Afghanistan as a medic. They had what Pam described as a "classic whirlwind military romance." They met in September in a coffee shop. They married in November. And he returned to duty in January. Dr. Platoni says that it is somewhat common to see soldiers in their early twenties, barely out of adolescence, with few life coping skills, marrying someone they don't know very well right before being deployed. This is a difficult set of circumstances from which to launch a lasting relationship.

During that four-month period, Pam and Doug learned to love each other deeply and to limit their conversations about fraught subjects like his departure date and dangers he might face on the front. Pam's grandfather, father, and uncles had military careers, so she thought she understood the life she had signed up for. Doug wanted to marry before he left because he wanted to know she would be taken care of should anything happen to him. This was as close as they got to talking about the dark side of war. Instead, they did what they could to "preserve the happy little bubble" they had for as long as they could.

They couldn't escape all incursions of war and fear, however. Doug had to update his will. His mother's phone calls were punctuated with uneasy what-if questions: what if he gets hurt? What if he gets killed? As much as they tried to tune out these bleak intrusions and substitute jokes and play, Pam occasionally got teary. Doug would tell her, "Don't cry. It will hurt my feelings." Pam convinced herself that "we waited too long to find each other, and the universe did not put us together to take us apart."

After he left, Pam tried to stay as busy as possible to keep from thinking too much about what might happen to Doug. They wrote each other letters and sent emails back and forth. They kept their conversation light by avoiding all talk of war and focusing on minor household events. Pam got enough war details from the nightly news and Doug, as a medic, saw terrible injures every day and did not want to talk about his work. Doug promised Pam "no hero stuff," and that he would "come home safe." Pam clung to that promise.

But Doug could not keep that promise. He was injured by two land mine explosions that occurred a week apart. The first one resulted in partial hearing loss, and the second caused traumatic brain injury. The military sent him home for a two-week vacation. Pam rejoiced that Doug was home, but dreaded the long, slow car ride that would take him back to the airport and on to his next mission.

Pam said, "Taking him to the airport the second time was harder. Unfair. We just got him home safe and then had to send him back to where he's not safe."

. . . .

KATHY PLATONI, PSY.D. — THE WARRIOR'S EXPERIENCE

"The warrior never comes home completely unscathed. He witnesses the loss of life for missions that may not be clear to him. The rules of engagement may change without the purpose being understood. There is so much human suffering the warrior sees over and over and over. He is called on to repeatedly undertake acts of heroism. And he feels guilty for surviving when others die," Dr. Platoni says.

To expose oneself to the possibility of death and loss every day (and for some, without an unwavering justification) not only harms the body but also wounds the heart and soul. For a warrior to come home asking "Why?" while feeling guilty for making it home is a terrible burden— for the warrior and for his or her partner.

. . . .

Living with PTSD

Right before he left on his next deployment Doug did not make any promises about not being a hero. In fact, Pam noticed changes in his mood and behavior. "He was angry at the world for getting wounded," she said. She feared he might put himself in danger to get even. "He was ready to wipe out everybody who was the enemy, any-one who might hurt him or his friends." After an incident in a village in which Doug lunged at some Iraqis who had been brought in for questioning, he started working with an Army psychologist who was based in Iraq and accompanied troops on their missions. Doug was only willing to talk to her because he believed that her experiences on the front lines with the troops made her uniquely capable of understanding him.

The diagnosis PTSD (post-traumatic stress disorder) was mentioned for the first time in one of their conversations.

PTSD is an anxiety disorder that can develop after exposure to a terrifying event or ordeal in which grave physical or psychological harm occurred or was threatened. Traumatic events that may trigger PTSD include violent personal assaults, natural or human-caused disasters, accidents, and military combat. Anyone can develop PTSD. There are three main symptoms associated with PTSD:

1. Re-experiencing symptoms such as flashbacks and nightmares.

2. Avoidance symptoms such as social isolation, feelings of numbness, depression, guilt, and loss of interest in activities.

3. Hyperarousal symptoms such as startling easily, feeling tense, anxious, and enraged, and difficulty sleeping.

Pam began doing her own research on PTSD. By becoming a lay expert, she was much better equipped to understand Doug's behavior upon his return home after his final tour of duty. She described Doug as having undergone "a complete personality change." He suffered from the classical PTSD symptoms: flashbacks, moodiness, anger, and withdrawal. Even though Pam knew that Doug's new behaviors were "the PTSD and not him," she was shocked by the magnitude of the change. Luckily, "Every once in a while I got a glimpse of the guy I married," Pam said. "We went through more in our first year of marriage than many other couples have in twenty years. If we can make it through this, we can make it through anything."

. . . .

KATHY PLATONI, PSY.D. — LIFE BECOMES A BOMBING RAID
WAITING TO HAPPEN

"Home-front issues are one of the biggest problems. The home front is no longer normal; war is normal. The warrior at home is angry, depressed, and irritable—living the war over and over with no spigot to

turn off the feelings and memories. When the warrior comes back home
he or she has nothing to do and his energy is no longer on life-and-death
missions. There is empty space, so the horrors come back with a ven-
geance. Flashbacks, nightmares, hyper-startle responses, social isolation.
Hearing a loud noise and hitting the floor. The trail of damage is a very
long one."

. . . .

Hitting the Wall

For three years after his return home, Doug was in denial about his condition.
He repeated the phrase, "Nothing's wrong with me, I'm fine" whenever his anger
or his withdrawal intruded, as if repetition could turn his statement into the truth.
Pam became adept at "walking on eggshells." She learned to read the early warning
signs of his dark moods and to foresee impending charged anniversary dates (the
dates of his injuries or of the deaths of his comrades) and to "give him space" at
those times. According to Dr. Platoni, partners often don't know how to help each
other. The patterns they established before one was deployed don't serve them
anymore. They are afraid to ask each other pointed questions out of fear of setting
off an explosion that would unleash a torrent of anger. In addition, the warrior is
reluctant to share his experiences with his partner because he might get deployed
again and doesn't want to leave her with frightening scenes of danger playing in
her mind. So the partners maintain a safe distance and try not to lose each other
completely.

. . . .

KATHY PLATONI, PSY.D. — HOMELAND IS THE FOREIGN LAND

"At first the warrior is happy to be home and to be alive. He is exhausted
and wants to sleep and also to experience all he's missed—in the first

twenty-four hours. Then he realizes that all those who experienced what he's been through are gone and that there is no one around who can understand and really support him. He feels a great sense of loss, grief, and frustration. It's also very hard to trust. In combat, people have to do what they say they will do or lives can be lost. Back home, people don't necessarily say what they mean and may pay lip service rather than speak the truth. The warrior doesn't know whom to trust. Home becomes the new abnormal, a foreign land that makes relentless demands about matters that seem trivial in comparison to what he has had to deal with in war zones—house repairs, taxes, schools. In battle the warrior only had two concerns: saving his life and the lives of his buddies. Here he has to juggle ten thousand comparatively meaningless things."

. . . .

Pam and Doug loved each other, but their home was not a safe nest for either of them. It was hazardous territory crisscrossed with emotional tripwires that could be activated by the most unexpected, incidental word or touch. They were living carefully, not joyfully, in terrible anticipation of explosions about to happen.

Three years after his military discharge, Doug hit the wall. Hitting the wall is a re-entry point that some soldiers experience after returning from a war zone. The wall is that moment when the soldier's psyche can no longer contain the mass of emotional turmoil and painful memories that have been accumulating. An external event occurs and inadvertently ignites that turmoil, causing a sudden release of emotional energy that gets expressed often as violence to others or to oneself.

For Doug, the wall rose up at work when his supervisor picked the wrong day to tease him and play jokes on him. Doug came home early and told Pam with chilling calmness that he had come very close to strangling his supervisor. "He wouldn't stop, and I snapped," reported Doug to Pam. Doug quit his job and for the next year, he worked on himself. He went to counseling regularly and spent time talking to other veterans.

· · · · · · · · · · ·

KATHY PLATONI, PSY.D. — THE WOUNDED PARTNER

"The soldier's dilemma is also the family's dilemma. The soldier does not exist in a vacuum. Everybody suffers. Families can only tolerate so many deployments," Dr. Platoni says. "The warrior isn't the only one with pent-up emotion. The home partner has been doing it all and may resent giving some of that back to the returned warrior. Or the home spouse may want to throw it all at the returning warrior, who is not ready. So many soldiers deploy over and over because it's easier than navigating the highway of strains back home."

· · · · · · · · · · ·

Shortly after Doug started his own recovery process, Pam began to slide downhill. For three years she'd taken care of everything—Doug, her son, her schooling, her work, and their home. She sculpted her life and her needs around Doug's moods. Pam said, "Looking back on it, I can't figure out how I did all this without burning out."

Pam was able to function at 120 percent as long as she needed to be Doug's ballast. As soon as he started getting help elsewhere, Pam's system collapsed. She started experiencing so much abdominal pain that she "couldn't see straight." She hit her own wall, and was diagnosed with stress-induced gastroenteritis. While she had been actively containing her emotions, her intestinal tract had quietly become dangerously inflamed. Her doctor insisted she take medical leave from her job. He told her that if she wanted to see her son grow up she needed to rest. Pam had no choice but to take this advice. She admitted, "I had been running on adrenaline, being everything to everybody. I pushed my body to the limit."

The Couple Dance

One special benefit of being part of a caring couple is that you have a compatible dance partner who senses and responds to your emotional moves. You have someone who can carry you when you tire and lift you up when you drop. You and your partner share both treasured and terrible times, and your presence in each other's moments enriches them.

Pam and Doug balanced each other, but after Doug returned home, it was a distorted balance with all of the weight resting on Pam's shoulders. Doug was dealing with PTSD, and Pam was "moving at a hundred miles per hour" to make sure that everything from Doug's mental state to her work to her son's well-being to the groceries to the laundry held steady. She sustained everyone else while she starved. And she kept moving quickly enough so that not even she was aware of the breakage her body was undergoing.

Doug was moody and Pam was exhausted. Eventually, silence became the only safe bridge between them. Doug did not want to burden Pam with his horrors, nor did he think that she, a noncombatant civilian, would understand. Pam, not wanting to do anything to incite Doug, and having very little strength left to buoy him, gave him more and more space. Eventually, to keep from causing harm and to balance each other, they just stopped talking.

It took a life-threatening blast to propel them back into each other's arms. Pam's illness made them realize that "one of us might not be here. That where we had gotten to is not where we wanted to be."

Becoming a Couple Again

Pam had to turn her powerful family energy on herself. For the first three months of her recovery she was depressed. "When I stopped going one hundred miles an hour I felt like I wasn't going anywhere. I felt like I had let everybody down." Doug was now the one to hold the pieces of their life together so that Pam could reassemble herself into a healthier, more integrated whole.

When Pam collapsed with pain or exhaustion and felt useless, Doug reassured her that it was OK to slow down and take her time. He hugged her and said, "It's time to just be you. Just relax and lean on me." Slowly, as her body began to heal, Pam started to enjoy being an at-home mother and found pleasure in reading books—an activity she hadn't had time to do in three years. Doug and Pam were recalibrating their relationship back into being a partnership of equals, in which each person knows how to stand alone, how to lean, and how to provide strength to the other.

Lessons from the PTSD Front Lines

Pam learned a great deal about PTSD from books, experts, and from her own experiences with Doug. Perhaps the hardest lesson Pam learned was to back off. She wanted to "make it all better" for Doug using the active nurturing methods she was so good at. However, she found herself to be helpless and, even worse, suffering from "compassion fatigue" and growing physically ill.

She had to learn not to ask but to wait for Doug to offer his thoughts and feelings. Pam's asking felt intrusive and threatening to Doug. In addition, he didn't want to upset her by describing the nightmares he lived with. He only felt comfortable sharing with other veterans, those who had seen what he saw, had experienced the terror, the rage, and the guilt, and still lived with the grim and explosive aftermath. At first, it upset Pam to be shut out of such a vital part of Doug's life experience. She remembered the early days of their relationship when they talked for hours about everything. She had to recondition herself to not feel excluded but rather to accept that he was getting certain essential help from his comrades and a psychologist and that she provided him with other kinds of loving support. As time went on, Doug began including her in his conversations with his veteran friends.

Pam wishes that more people understood what they and thousands of other military families go through. Extended families don't necessarily understand. Pam said, "We've been dealing with this for five years. Doug's family tells him that he's out of the military so he should get over it and move on. This is not a light switch you turn on and off. He's a different person living in a different world now. There is no way back." After multiple deployments the soldier becomes used to "a lot of do's and don'ts that are the opposite in the civilian world. Don't go into crowds. Always scan for the hidden danger." The soldier needs to reprogram himself to be able to interact in a civilian world. All the survival tactics that kept him alive during combat may render him ineffective on civilian turf.

Pam and Doug had to relearn how to be a healthy couple together. Her friends and family members told her they would have given up long ago. They ask her, "How do you do it? Why do you put up with it?" Pam tells them, "We love each other— for better or for worse. We have each felt exhausted and said that this is too much. But then we focus on what's important. We just love each other."

Postscript

"The warrior never comes home completely unscathed," said Dr. Platoni. We would add that the warrior's partner also suffers, and their relationship can be wounded in ways that require great resolve, continuous effort, and deep love to repair. When the warrior has post-traumatic stress disorder, relationship rebuilding becomes more intricate and demanding. Unpredictable precipitants can produce withdrawal and eruptions in the warrior who is plagued with intrusive recollections of combat and loss, sleep deprived, easily startled, angry, depressed, and adrift in a home environment that feels more foreign than the war zone. The partner, who was carrying the weight of the family and home during the warrior's often multiple deployments, must add caretaker to her list of responsibilities when the warrior returns. And she plays caretaker to someone who needs help but may resist accepting it. The warrior may experience PTSD, but the at-home partner can suffer from "compassion fatigue."

Pam and Doug, with the help of gifted clinicians like Dr. Platoni, were able to heal themselves as individuals and then sculpt a new balance in their relationship. Both Pam and Dr. Platoni expressed gratitude for the ways in which the civilian population shows its appreciation for the warriors' efforts and honors them for their courage and sacrifice. Dr Platoni emphasized, "This makes all the difference. It gives us value and a sense of meaning. We don't feel so alone."

The degree of harm, of course, differs from warrior to warrior. Some return home severely injured; others much less so. Whatever the degree, for military couples, a war-related injury may reside in one partner's body or mind, but its impact distorts both partners' lives, as well as the life of their family, and unsettles the balance they achieved in their pre-injury relationship. They need to reconfigure their responses to each partner's changing needs and to feel that their pain and hardship is witnessed and lightened by their community.

Part III
The Third Dimension

Regaining Equilibrium

Chapter 8

Loss and Grief: Finding the Self

There are three human emotions so powerful that when we are in their grip, all other sensibilities fade. Reason, logic, memory, and manners are obliterated by the stunning intensity of these feelings. Love is the most benevolent of the three. Love raises us up far above habits and flaws and wraps us in passion and delight. Rage crashes us down through the hardened crust of propriety and dignity into the core of our inner fire, where old and new wounds burn so hot we feel nothing but their intensity and our own insanity. Grief splinters us into so many pieces we feel as if we have lost ourselves. The only adhesive left holding us together is the force of the grief itself. Grief is so piercing, we long for it to end. Yet we also dread its ending because when it departs, so does a powerful tie to the lost beloved.

Love and rage seem pure in comparison to the complexities of grief, which emerges from love and gets entangled in rage. Where love unites and rage fills, grief marches us to the rim of the void and forces us to look at our essential aloneness. Yet grief also attests to our ability to love.

Grief and loss are further complicated by the fact that they do not occur only at the end of life. They run as currents through the entire experience of illness. With each change in health status, each new infirmity, each disappointed hope, both partners experience the loss of a piece of themselves and of their imagined future.

Trying to avoid the inevitable sense of loss and grief creates an invisible barrier between the partners and cheats them of precious moments of intimacy. While it is natural to want to shield yourself from sadness, the only way to achieve the necessary degree of numbness is to nullify the reality in which the sadness is rooted—and that involves erasing a portion of your connection with your partner. Yet dwelling on loss can blind the couple to opportunities for joy. If loss becomes the filter through which all daily connections with your partner pass, then opportunities for laughing together and for appreciating the splendor of the trivial get extinguished.

Each partner can learn to create a balance between grief and peace during the course of illness; and the surviving partner, eventually, can find that balance after a death. The consequences of finding that balance during or after the course of the illness can be restorative, whereas the repercussions of losing it can be tragic—as we see in the story of one of the women in this chapter.

In this chapter we meet two women who lost their husbands. Laura had been married to Morris for over sixty years when he died of renal failure after having suffered from Alzheimer's for three years. After his death, with the support of her children and close friends, she slowly began to "come back to life." Janice, a woman in her fifties, had a very different reaction after the untimely death of her husband from a sudden heart attack.

Laura and Morris: Falling Down and Finding Yourself

Morris, a brilliant, renowned scientist, liked nothing better than to be left undisturbed in his office to think. A strong-willed man who demanded that his need for solitude be respected, Morris tightly controlled the family finances, as well as his own feelings. He had little patience for unruly emotions in himself and others, and he exalted reason and order. When the volume at home grew too loud, at times he exploded, but more often he simply walked away. His family loved and respected but also feared him. They wondered whether his reliance on logic and avoidance of entanglements grew in part out of his experience as a Holocaust survivor who had suffered brutality and had been torn away from his family, never to know the exact details of their deaths. As one of his adult children said, "His life was about feeling safe."

Laura, his wife of sixty years, was Morris's emotional buffer. She was comfortable in the world of complicated emotions, especially those of their three lively children. She absorbed the inevitable family turmoil into herself and deflected agitation away from Morris. She often stood between him and the children, placating them and sparing him. Morris kept the family financially secure, and Laura kept them emotionally solid. She had been a teacher and an artist who never gave herself credit for her accomplishments, especially in contrast to Morris's achievements. She had a strong independent streak, but subjugated it to Morris's need for her protection.

One of their adult children described them as a couple: "They absolutely loved, hated, frustrated, and disappointed each other." They had periodic explosions during which his need for detachment and her desire for contact collided. He would become impatient and critical. She would become resentful and guilt-inducing. They would fight, withdraw, reunite, and kiss. Their relational patterns were not harmonious, but they offered the couple protection and stability.

Morris's unwavering intelligence was an anchor point for the couple. It was unbeatable and constant. Perhaps it was Laura's faith in Morris's inviolable brilliance that obscured her awareness of the early signs of his Alzheimer's. In his late seventies, Morris began to make financial accounting errors and would occasionally forget the topic of conversation. Given his brain power, he was able to compensate and mask his deficit. Then his driving skills started deteriorating. Laura noticed, but was so enmeshed in the sacred myth of Morris's intelligence and so fearful of his eruptive rage when challenged that she could not bring herself to take the car keys away from him. Instead, she colluded with his confabulations. It was only when he sent $30,000 to a sweepstakes contest that Laura began to acknowledge that something was seriously wrong.

Morris deteriorated quickly. In addition to Alzheimer's, he also had heart disease, bladder and prostate cancer, and diabetes. He lost weight and grew frail and more confused. Laura's anchor was adrift. She had so erased her identity in order to cater to Morris's needs that she became both unglued by his decline and fiercely determined to restore him. She had him accompany her wherever she went. When she couldn't, she left him notes telling him the date and time of her departure, her destination, and the expected hour of her return. She would join him in bed when he retired at 7:00 p.m. and listen to his jumbled chatter. She would tell him, "We finished the day. We managed. We love each other. Now let's just be together, quietly." She hoped that if only she worked hard enough, she could magically make it all okay, as she had with his other crises.

The Onslaught of Grief

There are many theories about the stages of grief. If there is a grief pattern, it most likely begins with some form of denial, followed by mental and emotional upheaval, which may end eventually but more likely softens and returns periodically, especially on anniversaries and holidays. Aftershocks of grief may continue indefinitely. We can safely say that there is no right way to experience grief, and while there are common- alities, every individual's grief is as unique and personal as his or her life.

At its peak, grief is overwhelming and as close as we come to death in life. Our attempts to give grief a structure that points the way to resolution may be a manifestation of an urgent hope that grief will run its course and, like a river, even- tually empty into something that can contain it. But grief, when strong, is not a river, it is an ocean, and it is all the single drops of water that compose that ocean. Grief roars, sobs, and whispers. It makes us numb or tears us apart. It obscures our ability to think while it plays endless loops of memory and regret on an invisible screen behind our eyes. Grief can turn us into screamers or statues. We can go to great lengths, as Laura did, to try to thwart its intensity and misdirect its truths. The more entangled the couple relationship, the more likely it is that grief will display its complications.

A nurse practitioner we spoke with told the story of a couple in which the wife's illness went from a slight cough to terminal lung cancer in six months. She had been the caretaker, he the provider. With very little time left to reorient, their lives changed completely. Perhaps because she felt the changes in her body and mind, the wife had come to some degree of acceptance. The husband flailed wildly, unable to accept or deny. His grief took the form of rage and blame at the doctors and hospital who, in his view, could either have done more to save her or let her go home without inflicting futile treatments on her. His perspective may or may not have been ac- curate, but the rage he directed externally put him out of step with his wife's inner journey and may have cheated them both of precious time together.

The Complications of Grief

For Laura and Morris and for other couples whose relationship has been balanced for years on a fulcrum of love and intertwined insecurities, the illness experience was complicated. Laura was dissolving under the physical and emotional stress of caring for an incontinent, confused partner and the weight of her own unnamed grief. Yet to admit to her limitations would unravel the system that had sustained the couple for sixty years and would mean that she had failed in the role she had forsaken all her other capabilities to fulfill: to make life safe for Morris.

When grief and other emotions threaten to overwhelm us and we are about to become either paralyzed or unhinged, we may be able to call on our imagination as an ally.

. . . .

TULKU THONDUP RINPOCHE — FOCUSING EMOTIONAL ENERGY

"In the Buddhist tradition, unlike Western traditions, death is not feared; it is seen as a pathway to growth and blissful rebirth," explains Buddhist scholar and teacher Tulku Thondup Rinpoche. "Life-threatening illness can rob you of clear thinking," he adds, "if you allow yourself to be overcome and blinded by the emotions surrounding the illness."

Tulku Thondup expresses deep compassion for the suffering of people who are ill and for the pain of their partners, and recommends that people use the power of their imagination to focus emotional energy into healing and peacefulness. He advises both members of the couple to shift the focus away from the emotions and instead concentrate on breathing and mindfulness through meditation. "Take a deep breath," he advises. "Think and feel that pain and worries are going away with the outbreath. Allow yourselves to relax and think about what is the best, the most important thing to do. Give yourselves the open space to reflect on what has happened. It can be amazing, profound, and magical that the shock and pain can exit through the outgoing breath, allowing you to create an open, empty, free space." In this free space, we are not

driven by emotions and can tap into our deeper wisdom and allow that
to guide us.

. . . .

Far from being in a clear space, Laura was being snapped in two by her emotions. She could not relinquish control, yet she could no longer manage. How could
she continue to hold both ends of this paradox? She began to pretend that Morris did not need certain care. He fought going to the doctor, so she stopped taking him. She became less attentive to fluctuations in his blood sugar levels. She began to explain his deterioration as the result of improper medication. In denying the
extremity of his condition and the depth of her grief and rage over his abandonment of
her, she placed them both in jeopardy. Laura was not being neglectful or cruel. She was
truly doing her utmost to perform her duty at a time when she was becoming increasingly incapable of functioning. The adult children stepped in.

Morris was hospitalized. After two weeks he was placed in a nursing home.
When Morris left the apartment, Laura froze. She shut down completely and hardly talked, slept, or ate. Most noteworthy of all, she did not want to visit Morris.
Her world had ended. Up until this point she had been trying to maintain her old life
and was breaking under the strain. Now she could no longer superimpose her wishes for
restoration onto the undeniable reality of Morris's absence. Laura sank into depression
and frozen grief. She left the management of Morris's care to their adult children.

Morris had a medical emergency and was transferred back to the hospital.
He stabilized, but was still dying. After much turmoil among the adult children and
without the participation of Laura, Morris was transferred to a hospice program.
He died within two weeks at the age of eighty-two.

Laura and Morris did not really have an opportunity to say goodbye. Many couples
don't, either due to fate or internal prohibitions. We are not taught how to talk to our beloved about dying. In fact, some may fear that discussing death may magically hasten its
arrival or at least introduce greater upset than already exists. Compassionate leave-taking
is actually a gift partners can give to each other. While it does not provide closure—a
couple's partnership is never closed—leave-taking can offer a bridge for the well partner
to continue living and for the ill partner to pass with a greater sense of completeness.

. . . .

DR. CAROL WOGRIN — WORDS THAT CAN HELP BRING PEACE

A couple can join in taking leave of one another without using loaded words like "goodbye" or "death," and without inflicting destructive distress. Each partner can first ask for the other's permission to talk about the subject. One may be ready to speak and the other may only be able to listen. Carol Wogrin, Psy.D., R.N., Director for the National Center for Death Education, advises, "Tell each other in words and actions what your partner meant to you. Reminisce about the relationship, about what you've done together, what you've gotten from each other, and how that matters. Tell your partner, 'This is how you have touched me and will live on in me.' The ill partner can tell the surviving partner, 'I have felt loved and cared for by you.'" Words such as these allow both partners to remember the treasures they found in being together, the struggles they have overcome, the disappointments they can relinquish, and the memories they will carry to their next destinations. These words can indeed bring some degree of peace.

. . . .

The Flow of Grief

Among the experiences mourners describe during the initial period following the death of a partner are loss of appetite, insomnia, headaches, stomachaches, fatigue, social isolation, crying, dreams and nightmares, speaking the deceased's name aloud, talking to him as if he were present, treasuring or avoiding mementos of the deceased. Mourners often feel as if they are in a bubble, separated from the rest of humanity by an invisible membrane. They can observe but not partake. They hear the stories of past events involving the deceased as if the words are disconnected echoes coming from a great distance. They may cry, but the tears do not provide relief. They only siphon off the topmost layers from the reservoir of sadness. They perform daily tasks robotically or neglect to perform them at all. In many situations, particularly after a long illness, the mourner may feel relief, which can seem more awkward to show than sadness. Some mourners feel a poisonous guilt over deeds done or not done, a guilt they can barely name. Sometimes mourners are treated as if they were invisible by others. In certain cultures where emotions are considered private, others may have difficulty making contact with someone who is so palpably distraught.

For two months after Morris's death, Laura was on the verge of disintegrating. She wouldn't talk to anyone, even though the whole family rallied around her. She couldn't sleep and barely ate. Unable to cry, she kept repeating, "It's impossible, it's impossible," without further explanation. She was put on antidepressant medication and eventually was able to get some sleep.

Luckily, Laura's family and friends were persistent. They did not leave her alone or allow her to sink further. Many days, they simply sat by her side. They spoke of Morris's death, but they also spoke about life—Laura's new grandchild, activities in the assisted-living residence where Laura lived, family stories. Slowly, over the course of two months, Laura began to eat and converse. She started playing cards with her daughters, an activity they had enjoyed in the past. After many more months she re-engaged with her community and began taking a pottery class. She recovered her artistic side and began to explore her independence, aspects of herself that had gotten lost during her marriage to a brilliant and demanding man. She continues to have episodes of loneliness and depression, but sums up her situation this way: "I miss my Morris every day, but I go on."

. . . .

DR. CAROL WOGRIN — GRIEF IS A PENDULUM

"Bereavement," Dr. Wogrin says, "is different than it has been understood to be. Before, we thought death happens and we slowly adjust, let go, move on, and reinvest energy elsewhere. Now we understand that our world changes, and we change. We are not the same person we were prior to the death." A more accurate model of grief is that it is a pendulum continually swinging in an arc between orientation to loss and reconnection to life. Dr. Wogrin explains, "We try new things, and that kicks up resistance, because having things be better is moving away from

the person we love. You don't let go and end the relationship. We continue our relationship with people who died. They live in us and grow
older with us." In conclusion, Dr. Wogrin counsels, "You can have a full
life and continue to mourn the loss."

. . . .

Janice: The Deep End of Grief

Janice's story was told to us by her sons. Janice had a very different reaction than Laura's
after the untimely death of her husband from a heart attack at the age of fifty-three.
Janice and Howard, both reserved intellectuals possessed of dry wit, fell deeply in love
and were married before World War II, but started their lives together when Howard returned from the Pacific in 1943. They lived in lower Manhattan and were New
Yorkers to the bone. They loved off-off-Broadway theater, six-inch-thick hot pastrami
sandwiches on rye bread from the Carnegie Deli, and the ancient artifacts at the Met-
ropolitan Museum of Art. They were fast walkers and fast talkers. They thrived on
manic cab drivers and noisy, dirty, congested streets. Both were unemployed Ph.D.
physicists competing for scarce university teaching jobs.

One day, Janice got a mysterious call informing her of an unusual job possibility. She put on her interview outfit and went to a sparsely decorated office in
a skyscraper uptown. After she responded to a few questions that barely tested her
knowledge, one of the interviewers told her that she had the job, on the condition
that she did not talk about her work and would relocate to New Mexico. Janice said
that she was recently married and could not possibly relocate. The interviewer asked,
"Your husband. Is he a physicist, too?" Janice replied, "Well, yes." The interviewer,
without hesitation said, "OK. He's hired, too." Within a month Janice and Howard
had told New York City goodbye and began working on the Manhattan Project,
a secret national project to build the atomic bomb, in the sands of Los Alamos.

Perhaps in part because of this shared upheaval and the strangeness of their
new environment, Janice and Howard drew even closer to one another. They spent their
days working in adjacent labs, meeting for lunch and coffee breaks. On weekends, they
went for walks in the desert terrain. Within a few years they had two sons and settled

into the rhythms of their community of similarly displaced ex-big-city scientists.

Janice decided to quit her job when her sons were in high school. Her older son challenged her decision and, in the rhetoric of the period, accused her of not being a "liberated woman." Janice replied, "I was liberated and working in a man's world before it became political to do so. If liberated means not being afraid to make your own choices and deal with the consequences, then my decision to be a homemaker is as liberated as any other choice. I have been a success in my career and now being at home is what I want to do." She immersed herself in cooking, cleaning, playing daytime bridge with her friends, and reading novels. Howard, too, decided to make a change and became a professor at the local university. Janice grew increasingly concerned about their lowered income and frequently encouraged Howard to return to his more lucrative lab job. This became a growing source of friction, especially as their sons were attending expensive colleges.

One Tuesday morning in October, 1974, the older son, Tom, got an almost incomprehensible phone call from his mother at his New England college. He finally understood that his father had died and he was to come home immediately. He called his brother, Jeff, at his Midwestern college and broke the news. Howard had suffered a heart attack while driving to his morning tennis game and was dead on arrival at the hospital.

For months after the funeral, Janice was inconsolable. She sat and stared for hours at a time. Her cheeks were always wet with tears. She wandered from room to room, picking up a book Howard had been reading, running one finger along the curve of his pipe, cupping her hands around his favorite coffee mug. She never went near his clothes closet or their bed, and most nights, she fell asleep on the living room sofa. She had to be encouraged to eat and shower. Her friends surrounded her with love, kindness, and comfortable conversation. Janice was unreachable. One friend remarked, "It's as if Howard took her soul with him when he died."

After six months of this, Janice's friends encouraged her to take a cruise and get away for a while. They thought that a complete change of environment, devoid of shared memories and familiar objects, might give Janice the space to reconstitute herself. With the same detachment she had shown for months about all activities, Janice agreed to go.

On the third day of the cruise, Tom got a call from a coastal hospital. The nurse informed him that his mother had overdosed on tranquilizers and had been flown by helicopter to their hospital where, after having her stomach pumped, she seemed to be recovering. This was the first of four suicide attempts Janice was to make over the next twelve months.

Despite psychiatric treatment and the encouragement and support of her friends and her sons, Janice simply wanted to die. She had always been boldly decisive, and death was now her choice. "My life was with your father," she explained to her sons. "You have your own lives now, and I don't want a life without him." Her sons tried to convince her that the world still held possibilities for her. They suffered out loud the agony of hearing that they weren't enough to keep her wanting life. She admitted, "I know that over time I would begin to feel better and that I would find things to engage me. But that's not the life I want, even if it were to prove to be a good one. I want the life I had, and if I can't have that, I choose death."

Though Janice had constant support from her sons and her friends, she could not assimilate it. Her experience of loss was so encompassing, it was as if it had become cellular, and her only way to extract it was to destroy what contained it: her life.

. . . .

REVEREND GWEN LANGDOC BUEHRENS —
HEALING IN COMMUNITY

Reverend Gwen Langdoc Buehrens, a priest in the Episcopal Church, grief counselor, and hospice worker, stresses the importance of drawing on the love and compassion of family, friends, and community when facing grief and loss. "Healing is the integration of the brokenness of the world," she says. "We can heal if we have the humility to acknowledge that we are part of many who suffer. When we share our stories and our grief as a community, we become a little wiser." She points out that the Mourners' Prayer (Kaddish) from the Jewish tradition teaches the community to reaffirm together the value of life, even in the midst of mourning. "You don't heal in isolation; you heal in community."

. . .

RABBI GEDALIAH FLEER — SUFFERING IS IN THE MIND

Rabbi Gedaliah Fleer, a scholar of Jewish mysticism, notes that the Hebrew word for suffering, "esurim," has the same root as the word "sar," which means turned. "People suffer," he explains, "because they are turned away from the light and can't find meaning." Pain lives in the body, while suffering inhabits the mind. Rabbi Fleer says, "Suffering is how we view the pain in our own minds and how we let our minds affect us emotionally, beyond what the physical inflicts." He asks, "Are we turned in the right direction, and can we see a purpose that is positive, a hope? If we can turn our minds in the direction of hope, we can mitigate the suffering."

. . . .

Sadly, Janice had lost her ability to connect and receive comfort, and death had become the only objective that gave her hope. Janice's suffering was quieted only by focusing her intentions on her own end. Her sons wondered for decades afterward why she became so fixated, so committed to this dire purpose. Why could she not imagine building a future for herself? They could not understand how a broken heart could propel their mother down such a lethal road. There had to be darker forces involved. They wondered if she felt in some way guilty, responsible for her husband's heart attack. Perhaps she felt that the pressure she put on Howard to give up the teaching he loved brought on enough stress to cause his heart attack. Perhaps this guilt was the toxin in her grief, leading her to seek punishment rather than renewal. Her only response to their endless repetition of the question "Why?" was, "I don't want any life except the one I had with your father." After a year of psychotherapy, which included some time in an inpatient psychiatric unit, no one came any closer to unearthing the source of her catastrophic grief other than the one she offered.

After two more suicide attempts, which left her sons in a state of unbearable agitation, Janice agreed to give them advance warning should she once more plan to try to kill herself. The boys understood that the only way they could prevent her from doing so was to have her locked up indefinitely. Even then, they knew she was intelligent enough to find a way to achieve her goal under any circumstances. The three had become so close over the year of tragedy and communion that they could not bear to imprison her or let her depart alone.

One day, she simply said to them, "It's time, boys." They sat next to her on the couch in her living room, and asked her one more time if she was sure. Without hesitation she said, "Yes. I have absolutely no regrets." Janice swallowed a handful of barbiturates she had gotten with a prescription pad stolen from the psychiatric unit and drank half a bottle of whiskey. Her sons sat with her as the life slowly slipped from her body. They had not seen her looking so at peace since before her husband died.

Grief Does Not Disappear, But It Can Evolve

Time does not heal all wounds, and sometimes grief, as we see in Janice's story, can be so consuming and protracted that there is no space left for living. But more often, we can make efforts to embrace and release the pulses of grief, which can help us flow with its force. We can allow grief to move through us without becoming our grief. We can feel its fullness while remaining connected to something outside or beyond the sorrow. Attaching to a belief, a friend, a community, a special place, a project, a pet—anything that offers a link to life—can be a portent of a time to come when grief will no longer be all we know. Reverend John Buehrens, former president of the Unitarian Universalist Association and currently a minister of that church, described spiritual resilience as "retaining the capacity to see life in perspective and to know that life, even though diminished by illness and loss, can be good, with real moments of value and meaning."

· · · · · · · · · · ·

TULKU THONDUP RINPOCHE — CREATING OPENNESS

Tulku Thondup Rinpoche reminds us that the root of our problems, and of our emotional pain, is the grasping quality of the mind. The mind hangs like a claw over a pile of worries. It is compelled to dip into the pile, seize clumps of anxieties and raw emotions, and squeeze them tightly in an attempt to nullify them through analysis and calculation. Instead of grasping, it is better to create space. If we can imagine a space so vast and boundless, our anxieties will barely cause ripples there.

Tulku Thondup Rinpoche offers three ways to create this space. The first: When you are calm, make a list of three things that you deem to be important. They can be actions, beliefs, decisions, or hopes—whatever comes from that moment of clarity and wisdom. Then when you fall into a state of panic and pain, revisit the list and let it remind you of what is available to you from your own calm mind.

The second recommendation is to talk to someone wiser, who is in a healthier state—a teacher or counselor. "When the mind is under the influence of emotions, don't say or do anything. Just let it subside. When under the influence of negative emotions, talk. Your chest will feel lighter."

His third suggestion is meditation and prayer. "When you believe in a higher power and receive his/her blessing, that's the highest place to go." He adds, "When you're healthy and happy, that's the time to cultivate a higher source. Then, when you are in need, it's easier to go back to the divine principle—like going home."

A major part of Buddhist practice is the focus on compassion, from which comes strength and courage. Thinking about not only another's suffering but the situation of all humans who are suffering and sending your compassion to humankind is considered a powerful form of healing. To move beyond self-centeredness, to offer loving-kindness to all, breaks down the walls that imprison us in our own individual despair. Tulku Thondup Rinpoche says, "Open up. Locks only keep out good people. Bad people will break in no matter what." He also appreciates that opening up may be very difficult for someone in pain who feels in need of protection, not boundlessness. He suggests, "Someone in a flood first needs something to hold onto. Meditate on something with an anchoring quality. Later on, you can open up.

...

DR. CAROL WOGRIN — LOSS IS DIFFERENT FOR EACH PARTNER

It is not only the surviving partner who experiences grief. Dr Wogrin, tells us, "Illness is not the same for both partners, and they won't grieve in the same way. One partner is changing in his or her body; the other is losing a partner. The partners may assume that they are grieving for the same losses, but they are not." If they don't recognize this difference, Dr. Wogrin warns, "They will collide." The ill partner grieves over the encroachment of infirmity and the knowledge that strength, loving relationships, and this beautiful world will soon be beyond his or her reach. Dr. Wogrin emphasizes that not only does illness bring day-to-day losses to the ill partner—energy, abilities, hopes, and dreams—but he or she also loses "the current form of the future." The ill partner's readiness to give up human pleasures almost always lags behind the illness's power to steal them. The ill partner may rage, cry, or withdraw. Certainly he or she experiences moments of panic and primal aloneness. While the partners' experience of loss is different, both can benefit from trying to create space beyond the illness to quiet the fearful mind and to connect to each other.

. . . .

It can also help both partners to consider what they think death is. To discuss your beliefs about the degree to which you believe death is an end or a continuation or a rebirth can become a way to commune together instead of fearing separately. In Buddhism, death is a part of life, so that the actual physical death is not surprising. With death the body dissolves, but the mind, the pure consciousness, migrates and continues. "Life is living in a guest house," Tulku Thondup Rinpoche said, "so why attach to the room?" Holding on to this particular life is not the ultimate goal. How you use your life in a positive, expansive, compassionate way is more important. Thinking about the impermanence of life can provide motivation to live a good life and provide benefit to others.

Reverend Gwen Langdoc Buehrens offered the belief that in some form we continue. "Physical death is a comma, not a period. We only know the music on this side, not on the other side. The sense of the person who died remains in the gifts of love that have been given and received."

Postscript

The presence of grief after loss is universal. The pattern grief assumes is mercurial and changes shape from person to person and within one person's experience. Grief may be subtle during the first year of a loss but explode during the second year or on anniversary dates and holidays. Some may mourn more by expressing emotion, while others may mourn through taking action. Those who experience a death within a long-term relationship may have more memories to mourn; but those in a short-term relationship may mourn equally powerfully the loss of the imagined future. For some, the pace of grief may be slow and calm. For others it can be turbulent. It can seem endless or fade too soon.

Both ill and well partners feel a profound sense of loss. The advice from experts about coping with grief is fairly consistent:

- There are no wrong feelings. Accept and acknowledge both positive and negative feelings.

- Give yourself time. Grief doesn't come with a schedule.

- Express your feelings and thoughts openly—to a friend, relative, counselor, clergy person, to a support group, or to your own journal.

- Let unfinished business come to resolution or disappear.

- Whatever shape grief takes, it is important to do two things: to experience and to express.

To know the full spectrum of human emotion, we must also experience grief. Grief is so pervasive that nullifying it can only be achieved at the expense of anesthetizing other feelings and detaching from sensation. But experiencing the pain of grief is not sufficient to move with and beyond it. We can only transform what we have first given shape to.

Wordless, soundless, invisible grief becomes a wailing echo that reverberates inside, endlessly bouncing from memory to absence, from yearning to loneliness. We need some vehicle for expressing and externalizing grief. Using language, music, sounds, or pictures to depict grief begins the process of shaping it into a substance that can be guided and transformed. Composers such as Beethoven and Mahler, artists such as Picasso, and poets such as Emily Dickinson have offered us versions of death and loss we can adopt to represent our own sorrow. The prayers, burial ceremonies, eulogies, clothing, and community gatherings that are parts of mourning rituals provide structure and invitation that give form to grief. All these modes of expression become the bridge between our internal desolation and the external universe waiting to hold us and help us carry our pain.

Laura was able to find that bridge and walk across it, to continue to live, and to mourn. The only bridge Janice could find was a conduit to the past where her husband was still alive. By becoming her grief and not giving it a separate shape, she sacrificed everything. For all of us, ill and well partners, there can be no harder task than saying goodbye to the life we knew and the future we dreamed of, together. Perhaps belief in some form of reunification or return, or even in a shared nothingness, can provide a steadying platform. But even in the absence of such a belief, there can be solace in preserving and honoring the memories of what was.

Whether your relationship has been companionable or tumultuous, the advice of a thirty-eight-year-old widower who lost his thirty-five-year-old wife to breast cancer is worth heeding: "We move through life so quickly and unconsciously. So much piles up and gets ignored, including appreciation and resentment. But you can't ignore illness. It won't let you. Do what you can for each other while you are healthy and then during the declining days to create the peace you hope to find on the other side, in life or elsewhere."

Chapter 9

Hope and Resilience:

Discovering Your Strength

As you and your partner move through unforeseen diagnosis, chronic illness, or sudden injury, you may arrive at a place of despair that's similar to the endless "dark tunnel" described by Consuela in Chapter 1. This may happen at the point of diagnosis or injury, as in Consuela's story, or sometime later, when the initial shock has worn off and the daily demands of illness, along with the search for new equilibrium, drain you dry. In this chapter, you will meet Chuck and Robin, and learn how they emerged from that dark tunnel into a place of resilience and hope even as they confronted terminal illness. The following story was told to us by Robin.

Chuck and Robin endured one of their darkest moments while Chuck was receiving treatment for pancreatic cancer. After one of Chuck's appointments, the couple met with the oncologist to learn the results of the latest tests. "The treatment has slowed the cancer's progression," said the doctor. "But the disease is relentless and aggressive." Controlling Chuck's pain and keeping him comfortable and as engaged in his life as possible would be the focus of the coming months.

"They told us there was nothing more they could do," recalled Robin. "We drove home from the hospital in a state of shock and went through the motions of preparing dinner. At some point, though, we just looked at each other, leapt into each other's arms, and wept together." This was the first time Robin and Chuck had been forced to confront the terminal nature of his illness, and Robin described it as a moment of great tenderness even in the midst of their despair.

While Chuck and Robin's journey is the focus of this chapter, our subject will not be limited to despair. Here we turn our attention to hope and its attendant resilience. Hope can carry you through anguish, despair, pain, and suffering, and bring you to a realm of potential healing and wholeness. Hope is not found; it is created. And it can be created in the direst of circumstances. Several experts we interviewed said, "There is no such thing as false hope; there is only hope." To this, we add, "Believe in the possibilities of every moment."

The Conundrum of Hope: Curing and Healing

The difference between "curing" and "healing" is often foreign to those of us who enjoy good health, yet it has a great deal to do with what many couples experience when dealing with illness. When the illness begins, the couple naturally hopes that the armaments of Western medicine will defeat it. Some couples pursue that hope beyond the point of possibility. Some couples find that when external sources can no longer provide remedies, they turn inward and look to each other for sustenance. For even if they are not able to hope for a "cure," meaning the elimination of the disease or condition, there is still much healing they can hope for. This includes deepening the relationship with the intimate partner; the personal growth that comes from meeting new challenges; the expansiveness that comes from finding new meaning in the illness experience; the ability to savor completely every moment of togetherness; physical comfort for the one who is ill; and some measurement of fulfillment for both partners.

It is never foolish to hope for a cure and for healing. In fact, hoping itself can be healing because there is a powerful connection between mind and body. Our emotions, beliefs and expectations can affect our physical selves. This is true not only for the ill partner, but for the well one, too. The placebo effect is one palpable example of this connection. One's mental expectation about the impact of a medication or treatment can influence the body's reaction. A patient given a sugar pill instead of a real medication to treat pain or depression may feel a measurable alleviation of symptoms.

The mind-body connection can be a powerful instrument for curing and healing. Your body "knows" what you are feeling and thinking, even if these expectations and beliefs are subconscious, and this knowledge can have a profound effect on your physical body. This does not mean, of course, that you or your partner can "think yourself well." It just gives you both permission to hope for curing and healing in every moment of your journey together. At a minimum, hope certainly can't hurt, and it may offer unexpected rewards. Chuck and Robin were able to make choices to activate both hope and resilience as they faced the ongoing complexities of his cancer.

From Friendship to Love

Robin and Chuck met in their twenties at work and quickly became best friends. They shared an office and the same offbeat sense of humor. They became the center of a close group of friends and were always looking for new adventures and fun experiences, whether cross-country skiing, reciting comedy routines, portaging a river, or camping in the wilderness. Though neither was married, they were both dating other people and would discuss the ups and downs of these relationships. As time went on, however, each began to develop romantic feelings for the other, but independently made the conscious decision not to pursue a relationship. "I don't want to ruin a great friendship," they would confide privately to friends, though it was clear to all who knew them that they were falling in love.

When their other relationships ended, they still tried to deny what was happening between them, despite the urging of friends to act on their obvious attraction for one another. One day, however, Robin called a close friend very early on a Sunday morning. "Chuck slept over last night," she announced. The friend, still half asleep, said, "So what?" They were always staying over at each other's houses. Robin paused for dramatic effect. "And he didn't sleep on the couch!" she said, before dissolving into peals of laughter.

They moved in together and became inseparable, truly the loves of each other's lives. They had a small wedding, and the birth of their son, Sean, a few years later seemed to make their happiness complete.

Almost thirty years passed, filled with good friends, travel, satisfying jobs, and the joy of raising Sean and watching him develop into a fine young man who took his parents' wacky sense of humor in stride. "Remember, as far as anyone knows, we are a nice, normal family," read a sign posted on the refrigerator. After his retirement, Chuck planned to enjoy his newfound freedom through more travel and adventures with Robin. They were looking forward to a summer vacation when what appeared to be symptoms of gallstones turned into a diagnosis of advanced pancreatic cancer.

Moving from Curing to Healing

The frightening diagnosis wrested Robin and Chuck from their comfortable world and rocketed them to what felt like a different reality filled with hospital waiting rooms, radiation, chemotherapy, and a new language. "The transformation to this new world happened without warning or preparation," said Robin. "One day, I sat back and marveled at how quickly I had taken on a different vocabulary, almost offhandedly using words that would have horrified me a few short weeks before, like jaundice, bilirubin, tumor, and the complex names of countless drugs. I learned how to inject a liquid drug into a pre-placed tube in Chuck's body, performing caregiving tasks I never thought of as part of my 'repertoire'. It just shows you how adaptable we humans can be when we need to."

For several months Robin and Chuck clung to hope for a cure. They hoped that the disease had been discovered in time and that the treatment was working. When that hope was dashed, they could have gotten lost in the dark tunnel. Instead, they regrouped and assessed their new reality, deciding to hope for a normal life for as long as possible. They consciously created a space in which healing interactions could continue, even after they had given up hope for a physical cure.

"I took my cues from Chuck," said Robin. "After the initial shock, he decided that he was not going to let this disease get the better of him. He wanted to maintain normalcy for as long as he could. He had a phenomenal attitude and more grace and dignity than I had ever seen in the thirty-five years we had known each other. He was determined to live whatever life he had left, fully and with gratitude for every moment. Chuck had always been an 'off-the-charts' social person," said Robin. He was deeply engaged with a wide circle of friends and family. He loved playing golf, dominos, cards, and other games, as well as watching hockey, football, movies, and his favorite TV series. He wanted to keep doing the things he loved with the people he cared about. Most of all, he loved to laugh, a symphonic, full-body event that never failed to delight those around him.

Chuck and Robin developed a plan of action. Between trips to the hospital for treatment, they would keep the rhythms of their life intact much as they were before: they got together with friends, both in their hometown and on planned trips. He continued his outdoor chores, working in his beloved garden and playing golf with his son. "He walked the dog, mowed the lawn, and we'd rent funny movies. We made a conscious effort to keep the atmosphere in our home light, while at the same time giving Chuck the reassurance that we were doing everything possible to keep him comfortable," said Robin. "Chuck not only needed humor, he also needed to know that he could rely on me to be the one with the clear head who would ask the questions that needed to be asked."

One of Chuck's first reactions to the diagnosis was that he did not want it to wreak havoc on Robin's life as well as his own. "The doctors suggested that life was going to change dramatically, and the diagnosis was going to take over our lives," said Robin. "They were suggesting that I'd want to take time off from work. Chuck said, 'Not an option. Robin is going to get on with her life.' This was part of his determination to keep both of our lives as normal as possible. Even if I didn't feel like going to work, I felt as if he expected me to, because it would make him feel better. He expressed his love for me by wanting me to be engaged in my work, so he could keep his life as normal and independent as possible, for as long as he could."

Hope Is a Choice

Chuck and Robin, in deciding to pursue hope even in the face of an incurable illness, were making a life-affirming choice. Instead of allowing the misery of a dire prognosis to contaminate other areas of their life, they made the conscious choice to strengthen the areas of normalcy and love and keep their focus on healing what could be healed. The power of the fear that attaches to terminal illness is so overwhelming, it can easily diminish any potential for joy. It takes conscious effort to choose and cultivate hope.

One way to choose hope is to focus on the present moment. The feared prognosis lives in the future. The potential for a healing of the mind, the spirit, the relationship occurs in every present moment. Living in fear of the future does nothing to prevent that future from happening, and only consumes one's inner resources in the attempt. It is only in the present that you can have direct impact. The present offers you limitless opportunities for choosing to hope that you can cherish life, strive for joy, and deepen love. Even within the sadness of illness you can hope to find an acceptance of mortality, which can then spark a profound appreciation for the gifts you have at hand now.

Protection from Invaders

Much as Robin and Chuck tried to keep the atmosphere light, they also needed to protect themselves from what sometimes felt like "invaders"—those who, through love and concern, nonetheless added unnecessary burdens to their ordeal and misdirected their energy away from hope. "Once, after a full day of driving to the hospital for a round of tests, consultation, and treatment, Chuck was exhausted and feeling wretched," said Robin. "As soon as we walked in the door, the phone began to ring with calls from worried family members. I could see Chuck getting more and more distressed as he talked to each one. He said it was hard enough dealing with his own illness, without also feeling that he had to manage the emotions of others as well. So we came up with a plan." Robin took all calls and told people when Chuck was not up to talking. She also set up a weekly group email message summarizing the latest medical developments and letting people know that Chuck would call them when he was ready. "It was important for him to take control of these outside contacts, since he had so little control of everything that was happening inside his body," said Robin.

Another source of difficulty for Robin was those colleagues and friends who constantly probed her for the latest news, telling her how worried they were about her. "I learned to trust the sensations that were coming through my body," said Robin. "And I knew that these probing questions were more about the needs of others than about my own. I consulted with the local cancer society and realized that it was necessary and right for me to protect myself, even from people who are well-meaning, if their concern was making it more difficult for me as Chuck's caregiver." Robin finally wrote the following note to one of her colleagues:

As I recall, you were rather persistently asking me on Sunday how I was. You even observed at one point that I didn't answer your question about how I was and made me try again. I don't recollect what I said and don't know if it made sense and don't know if it satisfied your need to know... but I've been thinking about "how I am" since then and the fact is, I don't know and can't say. I simply get from day to day and hour to hour and am grateful that I still appear to be somewhat organized, balanced, and sane. As I think I said, I'm sleeping, eating, and functioning as best I can, which to all appearances is quite well, I think, given the circumstances. If I need space, I say so. If I need help, I say so. If I need advice, I ask for it. If I need sleep, or a drink, or a good cry... I do just that. Down deep I know that what's happening in my life and Chuck's right now will probably take me years to "unpack," as they say in social work circles... so I'm not trying to make much sense of it right now, not trying to be too analytical, just trying to get through each day relatively intact... and for the most part, I think I'm succeeding. Perhaps I'm fooling myself, I don't know (but I think not).

A lot of people think they know how I must be feeling, probably based on their own imagined response to such a situation. The concern or worry or whatever it was I heard in your voice on Sunday made me wonder if you needed to hear me say that I'm overwhelmed or not coping or falling apart or something like that. I'm not... but neither could I say that I'm serene or predictable or joyful—and being put on the spot to express "how I am" doesn't help, because there are really no words to describe this wild roller coaster ride... and I can't just turn the analytical part of myself on at will to think about it and respond in a way that does it justice.

By contrast, Robin said, "The people who were the most helpful to me were those who simply squeezed my shoulder and said, 'I'm here if you need me.' They didn't press me for details; they declared their concern and their presence." Robin described what she was going through as "treading water and struggling to keep my head above it while the weight of stuff is trying to pull me under. For the most part I didn't feel at all like I was drowning... but I was getting a little weary of being in the deep end of the pool... but on the other hand, the truth is, I'm a pretty good swimmer and ultimately, the water doesn't scare me. What I needed was an unobtrusive cheering section that would respond compassionately and quickly to an expressed need."

What Are Hardiness and Resilience?

In addition to choosing to create hope, Chuck and Robin had what psychologists call resiliency or hardiness: the ability to adapt constructively to adversity.

· · · · · · · · · · ·

DR. SALVATORE MADDI —
COMMITMENT, CONTROL, AND CHALLENGE

Twenty-five years ago, psychologist Salvatore R. Maddi, Ph.D., asked himself: "Why do some people suffer physical and mental breakdowns when faced with overwhelming stress while others seem to thrive?" His interest in people's different responses to stress spurred Dr. Maddi to embark on a landmark, twelve-year longitudinal study of highly stressed employees at a company that was undergoing significant deregulation and downsizing. "We found that about two-thirds of the employees in the study suffered significant performance, leadership, and health declines—including heart attacks, strokes, obesity, depression, substance abuse, and poor performance reviews—as the result of the extreme stress in their workplace," says Dr. Maddi. "However, the other one-third actually thrived during the upheaval, despite experiencing the same amount of disruption and stressful events as their coworkers. These employees maintained their health, happiness, and performance and felt renewed enthusiasm." The differences between the two groups prior to the upheaval led Dr. Maddi to identify hardiness.[5] "The research revealed that those who thrived during stressful times had maintained three key beliefs that helped them turn adversity into an advantage," says Dr. Maddi. "We call these beliefs 'The Three C's of Hardiness: Commitment, Control, and Challenge.'" According to his research, hardiness moderates the relationship between stress and illness and can act as a "buffer," even

---

[5] Interviews with Salvatore R. Maddi, September, 2005, and: Maddi, S. R. (1987). "Hardiness training at Illinois Bell Telephone." In J. P. Opatz (Ed.), *Health promotion evaluation*, pp. 101-1115. Stevens Point, WI: National Wellness Institute.Maddi, S. R. (2002). "The story of hardiness: Twenty years of theorizing, research and practice." *Consulting Psychology Journal*; Practice and Research Vol. 54, pp. 173-185.

when people have inherited vulnerability to illnesses.

...

THE THREE C'S — COMMITMENT, CONTROL, AND CHALLENGE

Couples coping with serious illness, whether as caregiver or patient, can learn to use the "Three C's of Hardiness" to moderate stress: Commitment, Control, and Challenge. Dr. Maddi defines each of the three hardiness attitudes.

Commitment: The Commitment attitude leads people to strive to be involved with people, things, and contexts rather than being detached, isolated, or alienated.

Control: The Control attitude leads people to try to have an influence on the outcomes going on around themselves, rather than lapsing into passivity and powerlessness.

Challenge: The Challenge attitude leads people to learn continually from their experiences and to view acute and chronic stresses, whether positive or negative, as opportunities for new learning. Hardy people do not "play it safe" by avoiding uncertainties and potential threats. Rather, they are motivated by challenges to learn how they can grow and change for the better.

....

It is possible to learn to acquire hardy attitudes. In fact, Chuck and Robin did exemplify Dr. Maddi's principles when they created buffers against stress. Their decision to focus on the present and maintain as much normalcy as possible was a manifestation of Commitment. Their efforts to thwart "invaders" were evidence of Control. They demonstrated Challenge by continually learning and modifying their environments.

Maintaining Resilience and Hope Through the Three C's

Throughout that fall and winter, Chuck grew steadily weaker and began to develop abdominal pain. Robin added "advocate" to her caregiver role, identifying their needs and becoming more assertive with the health care system. "I learned that it was not enough to simply ask questions," she said. "My responsibility was also to become more assertive with the system and the providers within it. When a doctor asked me what we needed, I said, 'I want immediate access to you when Chuck is in pain.' He said, 'Not a problem, here is my cell phone number.' So I'm really glad I asked. I also made it clear to our caregivers when the medication was not working and requested alternative ways of handling pain, which sometimes included dealing with Chuck's anxiety about the pain. At least once, I simply made the decision to bring him to the hospital for immediate evaluation and pain management, making sure we had a clear plan before he returned home."

Throughout this time, both Chuck and Robin developed their own ways of becoming more resilient and maintaining hope. Robin turned to her close friends and family for support, and found that her lifelong habit of keeping a journal stood her in good stead. "I used my time with Chuck to respond to what he needed, even if that meant discussing difficult subjects such as his funeral preferences," said Robin. "For my own needs I turned to others and to my journal, so as not to burden him. I wrote and talked about my own emotional struggles with my impending loss, imagining my future life alone, and my grief at watching him suffer. I would have traded places with him in a heartbeat." To help her wind down and sleep at the end of the day, Robin used meditation and relaxation tapes, as well as an occasional over-the-counter sleep aid.

Chuck, too, found solace and resilience in writing. He asked to work with a spiritual advisor, who helped him explore the meaning of this illness in his life and encouraged him to write about it. "Chuck wrote pages and pages," said Robin. "He wrote his family history, an essay about his philosophy of life and lessons learned, and a beautiful piece about what it meant to be the father of our son. He also wrote about what my life would be like, and gave me all kinds of permission to move on with whatever would make me happy."

A talented amateur photographer, Chuck also used the fall and winter months to make copies of his favorite photographs and frame them as gifts to his friends. "A measure of Chuck's grace was the comment he made during this time that he was actually grateful for his diagnosis, since it gave him the time to do what he felt was most important and express his feelings to those he loved," said Robin. "He would say how much better this was than, for example, suddenly getting killed by a car."

Creating Connections

Robin's personal faith was another source of support and hope during this time. "I believe that in God's good time, ultimately, this craziness that we call life makes some sense and someday I will understand it," she said. Spiritual leaders from several belief systems offered us their views of the healing powers of personal faith.

. . . .

REVERENDS JOHN AND GWEN BUEHRENS —
CONNECTION AND CONTINUITY

"Lack of spiritual resilience is often related to unresolved grief," says the Reverend John A. Buehrens, who, along with his wife, Reverend Gwen Langdoc Buehrens, ministers to a Unitarian Universalist parish. They emphasize the importance of finding faith through connecting to others during times of trauma and grief. "In a couple facing illness, each person will grieve differently and each will feel helpless and isolated in the face of their grief," says Reverend John Buehrens. "But participation in a community of faith is helpful because it is a recognition of our shared humanity. We are all grieving people."

In her work with couples facing terminal illness, Reverend Gwen Buehrens helps her parishioners to find faith in the eternal nature of the soul. "Our sense of personhood goes on, and the love we shared lives on in others, even after our physical death. I believe that we all live on in others and others live on in us. The people who helped form me still live on in me. I feel that my father, for example, has an afterlife in me. We find the meaning of our lives in the quality of our contributions to others."

. . .

RABBI GEDALIAH FLEER —

HOLDING BOTH LIFE AND DEATH

Rabbi Gedaliah Fleer, an expert in the ancient traditions of Judaism as well as in Kabbalah (Jewish mysticism), says, "The most important thing about healing is to say 'Yes' to all possibilities." That is: to do all you can do to recover and pray to be healed; and at the same time, to accept that this might be your time to die. Hope and peace reside in fully and genuinely accepting this apparent paradox. Holding both the possibility for life, on one side, and for death, on the other side—instead of clinging tightly to either possibility—opens up an expanded space into which more healing energy can flow. Rabbi Fleer emphasizes, "When I say yes to life and yes to death, that's the point healing begins." He echoes the distinction that other experts make, that healing does not necessarily result in a physical cure. Healing may be of the spirit, of old wounds, and of relationships.

From a religious perspective, Rabbi Fleer explains, "You are saying, 'I as a human, want to live, but as a creature of God I understand that God may have other plans for me. If God's plan for me is not to live, then I accept death with as much graciousness as possible. When I work to live and also acknowledge that death may be God's plan, I become an open vessel, ready to accept whatever is meant for me, from God's point of view.' Embracing both life and death leads to limitless possibility."

. . .

RABBI GEDALIAH FLEER —

THE COUPLE RELATIONSHIP AND HEALING

Rabbi Fleer also sees the couple relationship as a potential vessel for healing. "Each partner dealing with terminal illness has a distinct and important role," he says. "The well partner must be sensitive to what the ill partner needs in order to help the ill partner get a grasp on the situation and move through it." The well partner can understand when the ill partner requires "a time for a measure of compassion and condolence, a time to be alone, and a time to be held." Rabbi Fleer explains that the well partner can gently communicate, "You are right, you are going to die and I am going to miss you. But until then, let's live as best we can while accepting that we may not have that much time." The well partner can provide a secure, loving context for the ill partner to come into alignment with his reality.

In turn, if the ill partner understands the well partner's experience of helplessness, the ill partner can release the well partner from carrying guilt by explaining: "It is meaningful to have you here, and if anyone could make this better it could be you. But I have to find ways to heal myself. This is something that I can only do myself, and you can't fix this for me. You can give me the secure, loving space to do my inner work, and if there is anything else you can do, believe me, I'll let you know."

. . . .

Transformation and Growth

Chuck's decision to work with a clinical spiritual care specialist reflects a growing trend among people with cancer and other life-threatening diseases to plumb the deeper meaning of their illness in order to discover the opportunities for transformation, personal growth, and emotional healing.

· · · · · · · · · · ·

HELEN BATTLER — THE POTENTIAL OF ILLNESS TO TRANSFORM

Helen J. Battler, M.Div., describes her work as a spiritual care specialist
as premised on the belief that "any challenge that life throws at us—even
if it appears with bared teeth and claws and throws us to our knees—is
a crucible out of which we can evolve and be transformed. My goal is to
help my patients turn what they believe is their greatest enemy into their
greatest teacher."

Grounded in Jungian psychology with training in divinity and clinical
pastoral counseling, Battler works with dreams and images to help her
patients connect to the wisdom of their deeper selves. She encourages
her patients to use dreams and images that occur to them as clues to
what is most important in their lives, and to write about their experiences from that perspective. "Each image that comes forward is the prescription, the 'soul medicine' that is unique to that patient, and gives a
clue as to what is needed," she says. "I ask patients to imagine a place in
nature that calls to them. We all have such a place we can think of." One
cancer patient, for example, kept coming up with images of watering
her garden. "This was her medicine. We explored her image in depth
and she realized that she felt whole when she was in her garden, caring
for her flowers in this way. I advised her to breathe in the fresh air as she
watered, and know that she is watering and nurturing something in her
own being as she cares for her flowers."

Other patients, like Chuck, explore the images that arise as inspiration to
write their life philosophies, stories, and messages for loved ones. "How
do I live with the cancer without it crushing me into despair, anxiety, and
fear?" Ms. Battler asks patients like Chuck to consider. "For couples, this
means living in the present moment and becoming alive to every experience, to dive into the cancer and use it as a way to transform as a couple;
to realize that life is impermanent and every change, even illness, has the
potential to help us become whole as individuals and as a couple."

· · ·

HELEN BATTLER — REMOVING THE SILENT ROCKS

One way to achieve wholeness and a deeper connection is to engage in counseling, both individually and as a couple, to uncover what Battler describes as the "silent rocks" that are in all relationships. "Those stumbling points that were there before the illness become magnified hundreds of times after illness strikes and can cause acute heart pain," she says. "Use dreams and images to uncover the silent rocks in your inner world as a couple, and then trust your instincts, with the help of a counselor, to uncover clues about what you must do, as if they were bread crumbs leading you through a mysterious forest. Every relationship has elements that are no longer needed. Let the disease be used to clear out and eliminate what needs to go."

. . . .

Through his own spiritual care journey, Chuck was able to focus on what was important in his life: writing messages to his son, connecting with Robin and his close friends with words and pictures, appreciating and living in each moment fully, and ultimately deciding how he wanted to face the end of his life. "Couples can together make the cancer into a story that changes their lives," said Battler. "Every crucible has the potential for gold, so that even at the end of life, with our last breath, we can say, 'I have truly lived.'"

Death as Part of Life

With the coming of spring, it became clear that Chuck would soon need more intensive pain management as the cancer took over more and more of his body. He and Robin once again took some measure of control over their situation, defining yet another hope: to die at home. "Chuck decided that he wanted to end his life at home, surrounded by the people and things that were familiar to him. Our palliative care nurse told us that we could have a hospital bed, commode, and other equipment, as well as round-the-clock nursing to provide pain relief and allow me some time to sleep," said Robin.

During this period, Robin made the decision to stay home full time to be with Chuck. "He needed 24/7 care, and I decided that I was going to be the primary caretaker. There was no way I was going to let a nurse sit with him when time was running out for both of us. We needed to be together. I also called our son, and we decided together that it would be best if he came home for the last few weeks to be with his dad."

During the last three weeks of his life, Chuck was able to fulfill his last hope. "He knew he was dying but was determined to be a part of our family life," said Robin. "He sat and chatted with us, playing dominos, although he was losing his vision. We had the hospital bed near the kitchen, so he could hear us preparing meals and talking, even as he slipped into a coma. His nearness also made it possible for us to hear the change in his breathing that signaled the end. We sat with him and told him we loved him, and gave him permission to go. Sean had read some of his writing and was able to tell his dad how much it meant to him. The fight was over. Chuck needed to be released from this awful struggle."

The availability of at-home palliative care made a tremendous difference to the family, said Robin. "Chuck was able to die in peace and quiet, not hooked up to whirring machines, in his familiar surroundings, and with the people he loved. I had overnight nursing support, was trained to give medication when necessary, and throughout the process I had professionals telling me that what he was going through was normal and natural. It was a sense of harmony to have Chuck die with us, in the life that he lived."

Several experts with whom we spoke praised Chuck's determination to take some measure of control over his death. "We have removed the process of death so far from the process of life that it is hard to recognize it as connected," said the Reverend Canon Nancy Adams, M.Div., Anglican priest. "I have seen so many of my parishioners go through this final frontier in impersonal hospital rooms, connected to machines, and I don't think we were ever meant to die that way. When there is enough support for death to occur at home, it can make for a more personal and intimate experience."

Postscript

Once the doctor gives a name to the serious illness and prescribes a course of action, it is relatively easy to abdicate autonomy, self-knowledge, and hope to the doctor's authority. Many couples dealing with illness choose to follow the prescribed route with no detours and no philosophizing. They want medication, not meaning. They place their hope on the doctor's shoulders and ride unquestioningly on her instructions to the finish line. This approach may offer security and direction, and even some hope, and it may be what is best for some couples.

Robin and Chuck showed us an alternative approach: They consciously created every step of their ride, and they chose hope. They knew the finish line was around the bend, but they did not spend their precious minutes together calculating its proximity. They defined what their experience of illness and dying was to be. In doing so, they continually lived on hope—that they would find connection, laughter, comfort, and finally a loving death. Whether you choose to create your own hope or to find it in your doctor's eyes, hope can, and must, exist even in the midst of despair. As Anne Frank wrote in her diary, "Where there is hope there is life."

Here are some of the experts' suggestions for achieving hope and resilience:

- Believe in the possibilities of every moment. Hope is not found; it is created. There is no such thing as false hope; there is only hope.

- Be clear with well-meaning friends about what is and is not helpful to both caregiver and patient. Send e-mails about the patient's condition instead of answering multiple phone calls. Gently tell friends that probing questions are not helpful—you will share the information that is important for them to know.

- Use the "Three C's of Hardiness" to moderate stress:

  - **Commitment**: Be involved with people, things, and contexts rather than being detached, isolated, or alienated.

  - **Control**: Work to have an influence on the outcomes going on around you, rather than lapsing into passivity and powerlessness.

- **Challenge**: Learn continually from your experiences, and view acute and chronic stresses, whether positive or negative, as opportunities for new learning.

• Explore spirituality and faith. Both patient and caregiver may find solace in working with a spiritual advisor or finding a spiritual community for support.

• Write for strength: Chuck found healing in working with a spiritual advisor to chronicle his life story, his hopes, dreams and beliefs, and his messages to his son.

• With the help of an advisor or counselor, use dreams and images to uncover the silent rocks in your inner world as a couple. Then, trusting your instincts, discover the clues about what you must do, as if they were bread crumbs leading you through a mysterious forest. Every relationship has elements that are no longer needed. Let the disease be used to clear out and eliminate what needs to go.

Chapter 10

Intimacy: To Touch or Not to Touch

Whether you choose to stay together as a couple after the injury, illness, or medical catastrophe depends on many factors, including the longevity of your relationship and the depth of your connection to each other—the "glue holding the relationship together." If the "glue" is strong enough and you do stay together, however, nothing remains the same. The medical condition of the ill or injured partner affects every aspect of your lives together, including intimacy and sexuality. Side effects of certain medications can also reduce libido and affect sexuality (so it is important to discuss with your doctor any sexual problems that are of concern to you and your partner). While it may be very difficult to talk directly to each other about your sexual needs and fears (and in fact, you may never have done so in your pre-illness life), there are practical, incremental steps you can take to reconstruct your intimate relationship.

. . . .

JULIETTA APPLETON — IT'S NOT JUST ABOUT THE ORGASM

"We've all been raised on the 'insert penis into vagina, shake gently' concept of sexuality, but that's baloney," says Julietta Appleton, a health educator in human sexuality and a certified hypnotherapist. "The best way to approach intimacy and sexuality when one partner is injured or ill is to go slowly and not be fixated on intercourse. It's not just about the orgasm."

Appleton advises couples to expand their definition of making love to include cuddling and sexual touch that provides pleasure to both partners and does not necessarily lead to intercourse or orgasm. She advises reframing the meaning of sex in your relationship to include exploration of each other's bodies without a goal in mind. "One couple I know arranges 'sleepover' snuggle dates, even though they can't sleep together because she's in pain. He'll massage her back to help her fall asleep."

· · · · · · · · · · ·

In Chapter 2 we met Emily, who suffered from a mysterious chronic pain condition, and her husband Wayne. Emily's entire world had shrunk to two points: pain and less pain. Sexual desire did not even register. However, she did want to be close to Wayne, and she needed his comfort. One of the most intimate things Wayne did for Emily was to simply stroke her hair, rub her feet, and read *Alice in Wonderland* aloud to her until she fell asleep.

· · · · · · · · · · ·

JULIETTA APPLETON — TALKING ABOUT SEX

If couples feel too uncomfortable to engage in any form of intimacy for two weeks or more, it can be difficult to restart the sexual relationship, cautions Appleton, because they may begin to feel like siblings to each other, and an "incest taboo" sets in. Honest communication is always important, but especially when this kind of discomfort is present. "Couples should try to have awareness and discuss what sex means to them," says Appleton. "Making babies is just one definition, and sex does not have to be goal-oriented. One way of doing this is saying, 'I love you and just want to hold you,' recognizing that when someone is sick, sex becomes one of the least important things."

· · · · · · · · · · ·

For some couples, talking about sex is the greatest taboo. They feel more comfortable silently, blindly groping each other rather than putting their sexual desires into words. Illness forces new forms and new directions of communication, as we learned in Chapter 3. Illness invalidates the couples' assumptions about how they will move through the day and plan for the future. Your sexual repertoire before the illness is also upended. The acrobatics you both may have enjoyed may no longer be physically possible. Even intercourse may become impossible. When a couple can no longer rely on habit to drive their sexual contact, it becomes imperative to talk.

Many men and women experience performance anxiety about sex, and it is important to let go of that, advised Appleton. "It helps to use phrases like, 'May I?' 'Does this feel good?' 'Do you want me to stop?' 'Tell me if you like this.' It can also be sexy and flirtatious to say, 'I really want to kiss you.' 'May I touch you here?' 'How about here?'"

Better Intimacy with Illness?

Frances from Chapter 3, who suffered from severe fibromyalgia, had spent years in couples therapy with Ted and both had learned to "speak the unspeakable." One of the areas that was "unspeakable" in their relationship was their sexual intimacy. They had different styles and rhythms, which made their sexual contact awkward but not unpleasant enough to break through the silence barrier.

As Frances became more disabled, she grew more sensitive to touch, and most touch produced more pain. Ted could no longer know what part of her body was safe to touch, what kind of touch would be soothing, and especially what kind of arousal might be satisfying. Ted's attempts at physical contact were often met with a groan. It didn't take long before Ted retreated and avoided touching her entirely. Frances, however, deeply needed to feel connected to Ted, emotionally and physically. She also needed to feel that she was still attractive, even though pain had quashed much of her physicality. They were in a self-defeating spiral.

Finally they began to use the lessons they had learned in therapy to begin to talk openly about what had happened to their sexual relationship. The set aside a quiet time and made sure there would be no interruptions. They spoke to each other with truth but without blame. They "owned" their needs and disappointments and did not blame each other for causing the sexual rift.

For the first time, provoked by illness, they told each other what aroused them, what they longed for, and what fantasies they had. They set up ground rules for intimate contact. They agreed that Ted would ask before he touched Frances, and that Frances would invite Ted to touch her when she felt well enough. They also agreed that Frances could touch Ted anywhere, any time, and give him sexual pleasure (without intercourse, which was too painful). They spoke about ways of being close and intimate without arousal—holding hands, cuddling, looking into each other's eyes in silence, and saying, "I love you." Frances and Ted wound up having a more satisfying, more intimate relationship after the illness than before.

The Power of Touch

"There are other ways to stay connected and to maintain the awareness of your sexual relationship, even if you are not acting on it in a way that you are used to," said Appleton. Touching is one way. Research has shown that babies need touch in order to thrive. That need does not go away when we become adults. Touching your partner can provide comfort and even some relief from pain and stress. Various studies and experiments show the simple act of touching another person frequently results in physical benefits such as slowing the heart rate, dropping blood pressure, reducing pain, enhancing immune system function, improving wound healing, and creating a general experience of relaxation and peacefulness.

One couple we spoke to found that simple touch made all the difference as the husband became increasingly mentally and physically damaged by early onset dementia. When he lay in bed unable to sleep, memories colliding with memories, shattering coherence, erupting in endless verbal rambles punctuated by shouts, she would take his hand and gently stroke his forehead or slowly trace his back and arm muscles with her fingertips. The gentleness and constancy of her touch quieted his body and his mind.

Likewise, when she was overwhelmed by the injustice of dementia and her own terrible aloneness, she would bring him into the bedroom and lay down with him on their soft bed. She would ask him to hold her in his arms. He enveloped her with a tenderness she rarely experienced in their pre-illness life.

Finding Connection

When illness becomes a third party in the intimate dealings of couples, the kind of sexuality they enjoyed (or struggled with) before illness changes. Illness is now in the bedroom, and sexuality exists in the context set by illness. Even for those whose illness does not directly interfere with their sexual functioning, sex—like roles, communication, the sense of the familiar future—suffers the impact of the illness.

Intimacy may take on new urgency when a degenerative condition threatens to slowly steal away memory or ability. Those who are embarrassed or threatened by talking about sex and intimacy will, hopefully, learn a new language, or experience the decline of an important source of connection. For some, illness provokes life-changing conversations about desire and touch that would never have taken place otherwise.

However, intimacy is not the same as sex, though they live on the same continuum. Some partners may find that when sex is no longer possible, connecting sweetly through touch and language is enough. Other partners may miss the active, unpremeditated sex life they had pre-illness. The ill partner can only mourn this loss. The well partner may decide that love is not enough, that sex with intercourse is essential. In this case, the well partner can either accept this enormous loss or seek sex (without intimacy) outside the partnership, as Abe did in Chapter 5.

Postscript

Illness does not have to mean the end of intimacy and sexuality. Illness does force physical and emotional change onto what might before have been an area of deeply private and liberating sexual connection. But that connection does not have to disappear. The couple, with consciousness and language, can transmute that connection into one that has more meaning, more playfulness, more freedom, more arousal, and more communion than they dreamed possible. The following expert suggestions were included in this chapter:

- Expand your definition of making love to include cuddling and sexual touch that provides pleasure to both partners and does not necessarily lead to intercourse or orgasm.

- Honest communication is always important, but especially when sex is uncomfortable for the ill partner. Discuss what sex and lovemaking mean to each of you.

- Consider the value of loving touch that is not sexual: holding hands, cuddling, looking into each other's eyes in silence, and saying, "I love you."

Chapter 11

The Practicalities: Making It Work

So far in this book we have focused on the interior world of the couple: the relationship itself, as well as the thoughts, emotions, and experiences of each individual partner. This chapter takes a different, outward perspective. While it is important to investigate and adapt to the "inner landscape" that evolves from an illness or injury to one member of the couple, at some point the outer world intrudes. Bills must be paid, and decisions about physical care, household management, and relationships with others demand attention. How to make it all work? This chapter offers the guidance of several experts to couples about managing the practicalities of illness and physical disability. In addition to focusing on financial and legal matters, we also discuss rehabilitation, health resources in the community, and the medical system, including complementary/alternative medicine.

The Family Legacy Journey

The time for couples to begin thinking about and planning for illness or disability is before it happens, according to Byron Woodman, Jr., J.D., L.L.M. "The first step," said Woodman, who is an estate planning lawyer, "is to determine what resources will be necessary to meet your needs." The resources you will need will depend on your circumstances. In most cases, if it's affordable, the best way to proceed is to meet with an estate planning lawyer. If that is not possible, you can start with an accountant, a financial advisor and/or a bank officer (there are also financial planners who offer pro bono services, as well as financial planning information available on the Internet). These are the people the couple should feel comfortable turning to as a "safety net" if and when a medical crisis occurs. "Get to know your team before you really need them," advises Woodman. "Don't wait until you have a diagnosis or until surgery is scheduled. Put them all in the same room and make sure they can work together, whether they are troubleshooting a problem or coming up with a plan that answers your questions. This is the beginning of what we call your 'family legacy journey.' Asking (and answering) the right questions will determine the quality of your life."

The target is to think about how to handle the unthinkable, and the way to do this is to break it down into smaller pieces by considering some questions such as the following. The answers to your initial questions will form a kind of "road map" to guide you on this family legacy journey. Some typical questions include:

- How do you, your partner, and other family members, such as children, relate to each other around money?

- How do you handle the financial decision-making?

- What is the plan for a disruption to the income stream?

- What is the level of trust and confidence in your relationship? (If there are problems with these issues, they are best addressed through couples' therapy before undertaking a financial plan for illness.)

- How do you like to receive financial or legal information?

- If you need long-term care, what are your preferences (e.g., nursing home or home care)?

- Do you have long-term care insurance?

- What are your preferences for end-of-life care?

- Have you prepared a personal statement detailing your wishes for distribution of your assets?

- How would you like to handle your assets if you die? This involves issues of estate trusts and controls—e.g., should your heirs receive assets outright or in a "time release" fashion?

Before Calling the Professionals

As you think about these questions, Woodman advises putting together some information on your own before assembling your team of professional advisors. You should come to some agreement about a series of documents that your team will then prepare, copies of which should be given to your primary care physician, your lawyer, and any family members you choose. To begin, you should prepare a family tree (including contact information), and an inventory of assets and liabilities. In consultation with your attorney, you should decide whether you want to have any of the following documents, and if so, what you would like to include in them:

- **Power of Attorney**: This document authorizes the person you (the "grantor") choose to perform financial and legal tasks on your behalf, including paying bills, funding trusts, and dealing with lawsuits. There are two kinds of Powers of Attorney: *Durable and Non-Durable*. Unless otherwise specified, a Power of Attorney is valid only as long as the grantor remains competent, so that the grantor can revoke it at any time. This is a non-durable Power of Attorney. On the other hand the grantor of a Power of Attorney may choose to make the Power "durable," which means that the Power survives the grantor's disability.

- **Health Care Proxy**: This is a *durable* Power of Attorney for health care decisions. Each state has its own rules about this, but in general, a health care proxy identifies a decision-maker who acts when the physician determines that you are no longer capable of making medical decisions about your care, including surgery, treatment, and choice of hospital. Because of the possibility of disagreements within the family about medical care or end-of-life issues (see Living Will below), Woodman recommends that only one person be named as health care proxy. "We also use a consensus letter, in which the patient requests all family members to confer and arrive at a decision by consensus," he said. "But if that is not possible, the person named as health care proxy makes the decisions. That is why the person chosen should be someone who will be compassionate and also decisive and competent."

- **Living Will**: This is a philosophical statement of your wishes for end-of-life care. "It is important for people to discuss their preferences with their physicians in advance," said Woodman. "This ensures that your doctor understands your philosophy and preferences about living and dying."

- **Long-term Care Insurance**: This kind of insurance pays for care needed as the result of physical or mental disability without interrupting any government-provided care. Long-term care insurance can have inflation adjusters. It can provide in-home care, or care that follows you around wherever you might be. It is usually less expensive to buy long-term care insurance when you are in your fifties or sixties, and definitely before you have the disability. "The premiums can be expensive," said Woodman, "but they can be worth it for people who can afford it and don't want to see their assets eroded by the cost of nursing home care."

Having the Hard Discussions

The kinds of topics described above are hard enough to think about, let alone discuss with your partner. If there are disagreements, Woodman shares some of the ways he helps couples come to resolution. "I look for the voice behind the opinion to help people be more understanding of each other," he said. "If we can trace the root back to the emotional need behind the opinion, and then we apply the logic to the situation—including budget, need, and timing—we can often negotiate a common ground." For example, a couple may disagree about allocation of assets. One person may want to give all assets to the children while the other may want to also give assets to surviving siblings. Once the root emotional need is unearthed—e.g., one partner wants to make sure his mentally disabled younger brother doesn't wind up homeless—the couple and their estate planner can together think of ways to ensure that this doesn't happen. A special trust may be set up to protect the brother. And if it seems like a couple needs grief or some other kind of counseling in the wake of a medical disaster, Woodman recommends appropriate professionals.

Sometimes, the issues just feel too massive to approach for many couples. How to possibly think about end-of-life care when the prospect of losing a loved one is so unthinkable? Woodman advises taking small steps at first. "Think of estate and long-term care planning like a decision tree," he advises. "Instead of thinking about 'whole tree' questions of death and dying, which are hard to face, start with easier 'small branch' decisions like power of attorney."

If your medical crisis has already happened, Woodman describes a slightly different scenario. "We immediately help the client gather key information, such as the likely prognosis, where the assets are going, who is going to pay bills and manage tasks associated with the illness, and how to set up systems so that the family can get through." When possible, Woodman also likes to meet with children of the couple. "If we meet the children before the medical crisis, we are seen as part of the solution," he said. "If we meet them after the illness or death, we are seen as part of the problem, because they haven't yet learned to trust us."

Dangers, Opportunities, and Strengths

Whenever couples begin working with a professional team of legal and financial advisors, Woodman recommends taking an approach that is a variation on a strategic business planning method called the SWOT analysis. In a business context, the executives look at the organization's Strengths, Weaknesses, Opportunities, and Threats. Woodman first helps the couple looks at the emotional, financial, and practical threats they are facing. He then helps them identify the opportunities they want to pursue and the things they are excited about achieving. He then works with the couple to enable them to identify the strengths (e.g., family support, financial means, the health of the well partner, community resources) they can bring to bear on mitigating the threats and advancing the opportunities. "The goal is to marshal the strengths of each couple to achieve the opportunities."

During the planning process, Woodman also advises couples to think in terms of three-year increments. "Looking forward, the couple and their advisors can see what has to happen during the next three years and use the estate and financial plans to achieve these goals," said Woodman. This is much less daunting than feeling you have to plan for a lifetime. "Working in three-year time periods means people can start planning sooner, where they are now," said Woodman. "This is how we empower people."

Rehabilitation: The Hope Peddlers

"We peddle hope; we're the hope salespeople," said Janna Zwerner, M.R.C., L.R.C., C.R.C., chief of staff of the Massachusetts Rehabilitation Commission. "After an illness or disability, people realize more than ever how fragile life is," said Zwerner. "Once you get that glimpse, you may realize that you are lucky to be alive, even if you are disabled, and you may have a new appreciation for what life can offer and its possibilities."

Even if you and your partner don't have that appreciation just yet, it is Zwerner's mission to help you get there. Because of advances in the treatment of trauma, more people are living after catastrophic accidents and wartime injuries, so that more couples are experiencing the disability of a partner than ever before. "Fifty-four million people in the U.S. have a disability that is serious enough to have a major impact on their lives," said Zwerner. Disability includes not only what is obvious, such as loss of hearing, sight or the ability to move, but also the less obvious: cognitive or learning disabilities that result from accident or degenerative illness, chronic pain, chronic fatigue, psychiatric disabilities from depression to schizophrenia, and dementia associated with aging.

When there is a catastrophic injury resulting in a disability, Zwerner emphasized the importance of early rehabilitation. "Because the brain is plastic, cells can change even in adults. In the head injury world, it is not uncommon for people to focus on the cure in the early stages. But even in the absence of a full cure," said Zwerner, "Rehabilitation spurs new learning, which spurs the growth of new neural pathways." In some instances, chronic degenerative conditions such as Parkinson's or multiple sclerosis can be ameliorated through rehabilitation programs as well.

Within this context, the hope that was discussed in previous chapters takes on a new meaning: "Hope can be two-pronged—you can have hope for some recovery, and hope that you'll have new ways to live that will be just as fulfilling as the old ways to live," said Zwerner. "We tell people who become paralyzed, there are a hundred things that you used to be able to do; now there are ninety-eight. What are you going to focus on: the ninety-eight or the two? There are adaptive recreation programs all over the country that can help people with disabilities ski and sail, for example. The world is becoming more disability-friendly; that helps with the hope." But, she lamented, there is still the class gap: "If you're poor, chances are you will have less depth of services and resources."

Finding Resources, Making Choices

When couples are coping with disability, it is worth investigating state vocational rehabilitation services, many of which are federally funded. In Massachusetts, for example, state vocational rehabilitation services provide assistive technology loan programs for people with disabilities severe enough to affect their ability to work. "Our state commissioner was first a client who broke his neck," said Zwerner. "He helped create programs to help other disabled people lead independent lives. Technology has now leveled the playing field in the work environment. For couples dealing with disability, whether temporary or permanent, the key is to find local resources," said Zwerner.

Home or rehabilitation facility? "After the initial crisis is over, try to avoid institutions for rehabilitation," counseled Zwerner. "Hospitals are not going to discharge you to the street. If someone doesn't take you home with the necessary care arranged, the hospital will send you to a nursing home. The social work departments of hospitals can make or break a person's life in this decision." The social worker can help you arrange your home care to avoid further hospitalization, depending, of course, on your insurance. If you have good insurance, you are usually given the choice of a rehabilitation institution or home care. Contrary to what some might believe, it is actually less expensive to provide rehabilitation services in the community—either by sending occupational and physical therapists to the home or by transporting the patient to an outpatient rehabilitation clinic. Zwerner said that people should do whatever they can to get outpatient therapy at home. "You are learning a new way of life, and it is best to do this in your own environment." For example, an occupational therapist can help a disabled person learn to adapt and function in her own kitchen.

Independent Living Centers are another resource worth knowing about. Independent Living Centers are consumer-directed, nonprofit organizations that provide services such as peer support, information, and referrals for people living with all types of disabilities. Their goal is to help individuals with disabilities achieve their highest potential within their families and communities. In addition, Independent Living Centers advocate to ensure access to housing, employment, transportation, communities, recreational facilities, and health and social services.

Preserving independence. When you are faced with the decision of home care versus a nursing facility, consider the advantages of a personal care attendant (PCA), advised Zwerner: "A federal program funded through Medicaid now provides for personal care attendants to meet people's basic hygiene needs. Most Independent Living Centers will teach people how to manage PCAs." Zwerner explained that the PCA program gives the disabled person autonomy and independence. "The well spouse should do as little as possible in managing the personal care of the partner who is ill," she said. "You (the ill partner) manage your PCAs; they work for you. The independent living philosophy keeps the disabled person in charge." In Chapter 1, for example, Frank made the decision to use PCAs to help his wife with her personal hygiene needs so that he could preserve their unique relationship as a couple. "To the extent possible," advised Zwerner, "maintain independence and keep personal care out of the relationship. Maintaining the human integrity of the patient preserves the delicate balance of roles within relationships."

That being said, Zwerner also pointed out that it is part of "the work of the couple" for the well partner to be trained in the necessities of personal care and dealing with medical problems, and most rehabilitation facilities will provide this training. "It doesn't mean you are going to have to do it," she said, "but you should be trained in case of emergencies."

Peer counseling. A valuable service of Independent Living Centers, according to Zwerner, is peer counseling. "We are all afraid of the unknown," said Zwerner.

"If you don't know how to live anymore and you feel like you're inventing the wheel, it helps to talk to someone who invented the wheel twenty years ago and can describe the possibilities for you. People feel isolated, but the best way to cope with disability is to talk to someone who has been through it."

Communities for caregivers and for specific illnesses. It can often be helpful to find support outside the couple relationship. It is not unusual for the physical and emotional intensity of coping with illness to leave each partner depleted. And when both are depleted, it becomes very difficult to connect to each other in energetic ways. In addition, there are times when one partner may not want to fully share the extent of that depletion. In these instances, it can be helpful to seek out a community of people in a similar situation, people who live with illness and can truly understand the toll it takes and who may have some advice and tips to share.

There are local and online communities for people dealing with a specific condition, such as cancer, multiple sclerosis, or brain damage. There are also local and online communities just for caregivers. An Internet search by illness or condition will provide a listing of these types of communities. These can be especially beneficial in that they offer caregivers a place to be understood and a respite from the activities of caregiving.

Integrative Medicine: Expanding Options

At some point in the course of every serious illness or injury, the question arises, "Are we doing everything possible? Are there other options?" This is the point at which many people turn to resources outside of the conventional medical system, namely complementary or alternative medicine (CAM) modalities such as acupuncture, massage, or mind-body techniques. Whether or not this is the right decision for you and your partner depends on your approach to health. In the interests of full disclosure, our bias is toward taking responsibility for our own health, which means seeking out all available treatment options—including CAM modalities—as long as they are proven to be effective and safe. We also believe that there is a profound difference between "healing" and "curing," as described in previous chapters. Working together, couples can embark on journeys of healing by using "integrative medicine," which combines conventional and complementary care, even if a "cure" is not possible. We do not recommend choosing one form of care over the other; rather, we feel that expanding one's "healing toolbox" of options by exploring CAM modalities in combination with conventional medical care is the best approach.

Xiao Ming Cheng, a scholar and practitioner of traditional Chinese medicine (a medical system that originated five thousand years ago in China), has been trained as a conventional orthopedic surgeon in China, with additional certification in acupuncture and herbal medicine. After many years of practice, teaching, and research, he has thought a great deal about how we heal and his approach to health.

He pointed to a withering yellow leaf on a plant and said, "What shall we do about this? We can perform surgery and cut it off, but if the plant is having a problem growing, this will not help. We can spray the surface of the plant with chemicals to kill any pests that may be attacking it, but that will not stop pests from returning. Or, we can nourish the soil in which the plant is growing, strengthening its roots and increasing the flow of water and nutrients throughout the stem, branches, and leaves. This will help the plant become more resistant to pests and disease."

If either partner has a broken bone, uncontrolled bleeding, a heart attack, a concussion, or some other acute problem, you want an ambulance, a hospital, and all of the sophisticated technology of modern medicine and surgery. But what if the problem is living with chronic pain, a degenerative disease, or a disability? Modern medicine cannot yet cure such conditions. Generally, your doctor can offer you medication and invasive treatments—along with the attendant risk of side effects— and advice about lifestyle modifications and physical or occupational therapy.

We believe that when faced with chronic or disabling conditions, or even a life-threatening illness, the best hope of healing is to combine conventional treatments with safe, effective CAM modalities, always, of course, with the full knowledge and guidance of your doctor. This is the meaning of integrative medicine. We do not believe that our bodies are like broken toasters, to be dropped off for repair with pills or surgery and then picked up again. We believe that each person needs to take responsibility for his or her own health, and that a caring, supportive partner can be an essential part of this journey.

As to the choice of which CAM treatments to explore for use in combination with conventional care, there are many reputable sources of information. The National Center for Complementary and Alternative Medicine (NCCAM), part of the National Institutes of Health, is a good place to start. The motto on the first page of their website reads: "Take charge of your health." NCCAM funds and reports on ongoing research to determine the safety and efficacy of CAM treatments. However, we cannot emphasize strongly enough the necessity of consulting with your doctor before using any of these modalities, and particularly before taking any herbs, supplements, or over-the-counter medications.

Postscript

Illness can too easily force isolation on the couple. Not only does the couple turn all their attention to dealing with the illness, but after a short while, friends and family members may start to drop out as they become uncomfortable with the illness and uncertain about how to behave. Couples living with illness need a community to help them carry the load. The community provides both practical assistance and emotional nurturance. Family and friends are wonderful, but the couple may need more than that. They may need special equipment, rehabilitation therapies, financial guidance, and emotional support from fellow travelers on the illness road.

Resources exist in all locations. The tricky part is finding them. Using the Internet to search is a good place to begin. A wealth of information is only a few clicks away, but do be discerning. In addition, couples can ask their doctors, hospital social workers, visiting nurse associations, clergy and religious organizations, people involved in illness communities, librarians, and city councilors.

While each couple will have different needs and will have to construct their own portfolio of resources, it is important to know that resources for all income levels exist. You don't need to have it all figured out; you only need to know where to begin looking. We hope this chapter has offered you some starting points.

Chapter 12

Words of Wisdom

Sometimes the words of the people we interviewed, both partners and experts, were so perfect and so moving that they stayed with us long after the conversation was over. What made these words so profound was that they seemed to express a shared truth that before the words were spoken was obscure or vague, but which, after the phrase emerged, seemed to grow in meaning far beyond an expression of one simple truth. If you sit with the phrases written below, these words of wisdom from the people who live inside the experience of couples and illness, you too may find they express something pure for you and move you to a different level of experience and understanding.

Hope

"Think like a person who is going to be around."

"Stay involved in life—with a positive attitude. Do what you always wanted to do."

"Don't ever lose hope. Don't ever give up. Miracles can happen."

"In a crisis situation, be reassured that things will be better, that there's a way out of the woods."

"Be as concrete as possible about the next step in circumstances that are uncertain."

"You heal better if you're in a better frame of mind. A lot of pain in illness is distress."

"We need three things to be well: something to do; someone to love; something to look forward to."

"You need to have something to apply yourself to when you're sick."

"Hope is vital, an important medicine. No one has a crystal ball so no one knows who will or will not get better."

"There is no such thing as false hope. The placebo effect is hope in a pill form."

"Simplify life and focus on the important—family and friends. Refuse to let the illness rob you of life and joy."

"Keep your sense of humor."

"It's never too late to have a happy ending—to revisit old ghosts and put them to rest."

"Hope is important: hope for some recovery and hope in learning and finding a new way to live."

"With disability: there used to be one hundred things you could do; now there are ninety-eight. What will you focus on: the two things you can't do or the ninety-eight you can?"

"Your life may not be the same. But you can have a good life, even a better life."

"Other families lived for yearly vacations. That's when they appreciated each other. We had to figure out each day, together."

"Friends' kids care about cars and fashion styles. Their life is all about stuff, and that's not what makes you happy. Doing and caring and connecting are what matter."

"Be present in the moment. Don't think too far ahead. Just live the day you have."

Getting Help

"Get help. It's OK to get help."

"Be honest about what you can do and what you cannot do. Acting out of a sense of obligation leads to feeling resentful."

"Weigh what you can and cannot do, and what you have no right to do."

"Have your own people to talk to—friends, therapists, spouse, coworkers. Have someone you can dump with—or use a journal."

"Don't get cocky. Respect your limits. If I do too much I become a puddle of pudding."

"Don't be totally dependant on your spouse. You end up with a spousal relationship that becomes parent/child."

"Love each other. Support each other. Don't leave each other alone in the dark."

"Don't beat yourself up over things you can't do."

"Help others. Offer your support to others going through the experience."

Caregivers

"People who need respite are the caregivers."

"The caregiver needs to seek support for himself—practical, emotional, spiritual. Think about what you need for the long haul."

"It can't be all about the ill person's needs all the time."

"You do the love thing and find someone else to do the caretaking."

Dealing with the System

"Question doctors about each decision."

"Be more knowledgeable."

"Don't do it alone—dealing with the medical system. Don't go to office visits alone. Patients should never go into a meeting with a doctor solo—bring a spouse or a friend or a relative."

"Be aware of when to say no."

"Deal with the whole. Everyone else in the system is just dealing with pieces."

"Family members need to get educated about the person's illness."

"When you are facing catastrophic illness, take a deep breath. Realize you do have options and decisions to make. Gather information."

"Your medical team works for you."

"With a doctor, be skeptical. Keep asking, 'Why? What are the options? What if we did the other option?' If you don't get an answer, ask again or seek advice elsewhere."

"We are our own care. We own the responsibility for our care."

"Get that second opinion. You are in charge. It's your decision."

"With the medical system, use all your resources. Get info, ask questions, get clarification, ask someone to advocate for you. It's your life."

"See what's happening in terms of your health care as part of a system that forces a form of dependency on you, instead of internalizing this as your own inadequacy."

Emotions

"Do anything to discharge stress, even if you think you're not feeling it. It takes a toll on your body."

"Be prepared to see behaviors, emotions, and sides of family members you may not have seen before. The deepest stuff gets triggered and comes out. Allies may become attackers."

"People react from their experiences; don't take it personally."

"Appreciate that each person is just holding on."

"Stay away from toxic people until you're stronger."

"Don't flog yourself."

"Sadness, if used in the right way, can generate compassion."

"There's an economics of energy. If you spend it on anger you have less to spend on healing."

Communication

"If the relationship is not good in the best of circumstances it won't be good in the worst."

"You never know when illness, pain, or trauma will happen. Couples should examine if there are any loose stones in the foundation of their relationship. Learn empathy. Learn different ways to communicate before illness or trauma happens."

"Invite people to talk about what's on their mind. Ask, 'What worries you? Are there things about this illness that concern you? Are there things that are hard to talk about?'"

"Shift your focus to what really matters in the relationship."

"Expressing feelings, needs, wants is not likely to hurt anybody. Do it authentically and hopefully. If they can't respond, grieve the loss and move on."

"If we have no contact with our inner landscape we will keep projecting outward onto the partner. And the part that gets projected is the part you don't want to look at in yourself: your shame, anger, vulnerability. You react to it in your partner instead of healing it in yourself."

"It's a rotten time to be taking everybody literally. Everyone is suffering. Don't react to little words."

"Find a good social worker to moderate. The illness situation puts people with a lifetime of issues into a pressure cooker."

"To say goodbye: tell what the partner meant to you; reminisce about the relationship—what you've done, what you've gotten, what matters. This is how you touched me and will live on in me."

"Silence is the ultimate communion."

Stress

"Life is complicated enough when you're well. When you're sick it gets totally unmanageable."

"This is uncharted territory. I don't know this road. There's no script. Everything is unfamiliar and you reinvent yourself every day."

Healing

"You can have wholeness without recovery."

"All one can do is stand by and receive."

"There is a randomness through all existence—viruses can mutate, evolution has a bias towards diversity. Illness comes out of this randomness. It is not God's punishment or a personal attack."

"Let the moment of death have its place in the room."

"Don't underestimate the power of touch."

"Every grief situation involves a recognition that this is a less-than-perfect situation in a less-than-perfect relationship. The valuable needs to be sifted from the bitter. Hold on to the one and let go of the other."

"Feel regret without making it guilt."

"There is a learning opportunity in all afflictions."

"If a person suffers enough he begins to look for meaning, and his consciousness is then turned toward a higher meaning, to a meaning beyond the self."

"Illness is as much opportunity as it is crisis. Ask: 'What is it I need to learn? About relationships to others, to spirituality? What do I keep and what do I let go of?'"

"Resilience is about having a spiritual life, a perspective that supports a wider view, a sense of something that carries beyond death; a sense of humor, even in the most horrible moments; supportive community; finding meaning in caring for others."

"Death is not necessarily the worst thing."

"We go through life routinely. Illness can be the jolt that can remove the dullness and unveil the potential."

"We've removed the process of death from living so much that it's hardly recognizable as part of the whole."

"You have to have a relationship with life and death to live fully."

"Follow these four things: intuitions, feelings, energies, images. They will lead you to the self-awareness you need to move ahead."

"Wholeness is the cure. Make this a journey that changes your life and the lives of others so that the illness becomes the teacher."

"Do we spend our time wishing the illness weren't there or do we find a way to use it for our benefit?"

"Illness can be an opportunity for the couple to let go of what has been killing them."

Intimacy

"Everybody is different and has a different perception of sexuality. Some people might not want sex if they're ill. Some find it comforting."

"We need to change the definition from sex to making love. Making love is about being intimate—sharing sexual touch that pleasures one or both partners that does not need to end in orgasm."

"'Insert penis into vagina and then shake' is what people know. Illness turns this upside down."

"Just start with what feels good."

Preparation

"Have your house in order—living wills, power of attorney, health care proxy, will."

"But don't put too much reliance in living wills. It's easiest to plan when you're in good health."

"Respect the wishes of the ill person. There are decisions it might not be yours to make."

"Know about finances. Talk about this when the person is still viable."

"Work through emotional issues as well as financial ones."

"Look at your nutrition and lifestyle and find ways to make it easier now."

"Get in touch with all the financial planning professionals you need before illness hits."

"Give your living will to your primary physician and have a heart-to-heart discussion with him/her about your wishes."

Postscript

Unfortunately, wisdom does not usually arrive, on demand, in a chariot with the word "Enlightenment" pulsing in neon on the side. It can tap us gently on the arm, or it can blast us in the face with a surprising roar. However it enters, for it to stick and have impact, wisdom requires that we pay close attention.

The key to gaining wisdom is to be open to allowing new perspectives to enter into the fortress many of us have around our minds and hearts—the fortress we created to protect us from emotional and physical assault throughout our lives. This structure may have helped us remain upright through past assaults, but illness has already seeped into its mortar and has already caused breaches. The shift illness compels infiltrates into our being, and what held us together in the past gets strained beyond coherence. At this point, we can either choose to fortify with sand bags, or to open up to new wisdom.

As the words of wisdom in this chapter reveal, new insights can be obvious, and they can be profound. We can change in our relationship with the medical system, with our partner, and with ourselves. We can learn what is truly essential and embrace that. And we can learn what is distracting and remove that. The halt illness imposes on our busy lives can give us the space we need to finally make sense of patterns that have entrapped us for decades.

Much of the wisdom is about finding something beyond illness and our own egos that brings us to a place of connection with a larger construct—community, family, the human condition, even the divine. So many of our couples and experts spoke of the surprising power that comes from rising above symptoms and making meaning out of the illness experience. Wisdom does not eliminate illness; but it can change the nature of our relationship with the illness experience so that while the scope of our lives may become constricted, the expansion our minds and hearts can achieve is unbounded.